2014 White House Tribal Nations Conference Progress Report

Table of Contents

Executive Summary

The President considers the government-to-government relationship with Indian tribes a lasting covenant to be nourished and strengthened. To this end, engagement, consultation, and interagency collaboration are critical to supporting tribes in building stronger tribal communities. In 2013, the White House Tribal Nations Conference focused on the newly established White House Council on Native American Affairs. The Council is responsible for coordinating the U.S. government's engagement and partnership with tribes in order to promote more prosperous and resilient Native American communities. This year, tribal leaders were provided the opportunity to directly engage with the Council during the plenary session of the Conference to not only voice their concerns but also propose solutions to strengthen the Administration's tribal policies.

This year, the President made significant enhancements to tribal self-government and self-determination. In January, the President signed an amendment to the Stafford Act which gives tribes the option to directly request Federal emergency assistance when natural disasters strike their homelands. In March, the President signed the Violence Against Women Reauthorization Act, which grants tribal courts the right to exercise their sovereign power to prosecute those who commit acts of domestic violence in Indian Country. And this November, the President announced the State, Local, and Tribal Leaders Task Force on Climate Preparedness and Resilience. The task force, comprised of tribal officials along with national, state, and local authorities, advises the Federal government on key actions it can take to support local preparedness to the impacts of climate change.

The Administration's commitment to tribal consultation and collaboration has led to substantial policy achievements and a much improved partnership with tribes. While much progress has been made, the President recognizes that we have much more work to do. The President and his Administration look forward to working with tribal leaders to advance Indian issues through executive actions that result in meaningful and lasting change in Indian Country. The President also looks forward to making a trip to Indian Country in 2014, a commitment made during the Tribal Nations Conference Plenary Session in response to overwhelming tribal requests.

Sustaining and Advancing the Relationship between Indian Tribes and the Federal Government

Establishing White House Council on Native American Affairs

To demonstrate the Administration's commitment to advancing stronger government-to-government relationships, the President signed Executive Order 13647 establishing the White House Council on Native American Affairs in 2013. The Council consists of Cabinet Secretaries and heads of other federal agencies and is responsible for coordinating policies across the government to promote and sustain prosperous and resilient Native American communities. Specifically, the Council is tasked with promoting the development of tribal communities in five key areas: 1) promoting sustainable economic development; 2) supporting access to greater nutrition and healthcare; 3) improving tribal justice systems; 4) expanding and improving educational opportunities; and 5) protecting tribal lands and promoting tribal cultures.

The White House Council on Native American Affairs convened listening sessions with tribal leaders at the 2013 Tribal Nations Conference. *(Department of Interior Photo)*

The Administration also continues to build on the Presidential Memorandum, "Consultation and Coordination with Tribal Governments," which directs every Federal agency to develop a plan to fully implement Executive Order 13175 ("E.O. 13175"). The Memorandum has led to unprecedented levels of tribal consultation. Key highlights of advancing consultation with tribal governments this year include:

- On August 29, 2013, Attorney General Eric Holder approved a Policy Statement on Tribal Consultation for the Department of Justice (DOJ).

- This year the Administration for Children and Families (ACF) established the ACF Tribal Advisory Committee. The role of the Committee is to advise ACF on programs and policies relating to tribes.
- On November 4-5, 2013, the Indian Health Service (IHS) conducted two virtual Tribal Consultation Summits to hear updates from IHS tribal workgroups and committees. These summits serve as a "one-stop-shop" to learn about current IHS tribal consultation activities.
- During Fiscal Year (FY) 2013, the Veterans Affairs' (VA) Office of Tribal Government Relations held a number of regional training summits with over 700 attendees in locations across the country to foster consultation, relationship-building, and intergovernmental engagement.
- The National Oceanic and Atmospheric Administration (NOAA) completed a new handbook entitled *NOAA Procedures for Government-to-Government Consultation with Federally Recognized Indian Tribes and Alaska Natives.* This handbook provides guidance to NOAA line and staff offices for a more consistent, effective, and proactive approach to conducting tribal consultations. Other NOAA initiatives include the creation of an internal webpage with a tribal consultation tracking database and an external webpage on tribal consultations.
- This year, the National Indian Gaming Commission (NIGC) reviewed its regulations with significant input from tribes and tribal regulators. As part of the Commission's Assistance, Compliance, and Enforcement (ACE) initiative, the Commission staff conducted 132 training courses and hosted 462 technical assistance events. In FY 2013, 81 percent of all tribes participated in some form of training or technical assistance, with a total of 4,332 attendees.

Advancing Tribal Sovereignty

The United States recognizes a unique legal and political relationship with Federally-recognized tribes. This relationship is set forth in the Constitution of the United States, treaties, statutes, Executive Orders, administrative rules and regulations, and judicial decisions. The foregoing policies promoting self-determination seek to bolster tribal institutions and help American Indians and Alaska Natives (AI/AN) in their efforts to rebuild as prosperous native nations.

Violence Against Women Act

On March 7, 2013, President Obama signed the Violence Against Women Reauthorization Act of 2013 (VAWA 2013). This law contains provisions that significantly improve the safety of Native women and allow federal and tribal law enforcement agencies to hold perpetrators of domestic violence accountable for their crimes. Many of the critical provisions codified in VAWA were drawn from DOJ's July 2011 proposal for new federal legislation to combat violence against AI/AN women. The tribal provisions in VAWA address legal gaps by: (1) recognizing tribes' power to exercise concurrent criminal jurisdiction over domestic violence cases in certain circumstances, regardless of whether the defendant is Indian or non-Indian; (2) clarifying that tribal courts have full civil jurisdiction to issue and enforce protection orders involving any person, Indian or non-Indian; (3) creating new Federal statutes to address crimes of violence, such as strangulation, committed against a spouse or intimate partner; and (4) providing more robust Federal sentences for certain acts of domestic violence in Indian Country.

On June 14, 2013, DOJ filed a notice in the Federal Register proposing procedures for Indian tribes that wish to participate in the voluntary pilot project described in section 908(b)(2) of VAWA 2013. The notice invited public comment on the proposed procedures and solicited interest from tribes wishing to participate in the Pilot Project. Tribes approved for participation in the Pilot Project were announced in February of 2014: the Pascua Yaqui tribe, the Umatilla Tribe, and the Tulalip Tribe. All are authorized to implement the special domestic violence criminal jurisdiction provisions of the Act in advance of the effective date on March 7, 2015.

Strengthened Collaboration with Tribal Leaders on Disaster Relief and Climate Resilience in Indian Country

The Sandy Recovery Improvement Act of 2013

The Robert T. Stafford Disaster Relief and Emergency Assistance Act (Stafford Act) authorizes the President to make certain programs of assistance available to supplement tribal, state, territorial, and local efforts to respond to and recover from an incident that exceeds all available resources and overwhelms the tribal, state, territorial, and local governments. On January 29, 2013, the President strengthened the Federal Emergency Management Agency's (FEMA) relationship with tribal governments by signing the Sandy Recovery Improvement Act of 2013 (SRIA). SRIA amended the Stafford Act to provide Federally-recognized tribal governments the option to request a Presidential emergency or major disaster declaration independent of a state. Previously, tribal governments were required to seek disaster assistance through a state's declaration request. FEMA is developing guidance that describes the process for tribes to directly request Presidential disaster declarations, and will consult with tribal governments on its development.

The State, Local and Tribal Leaders Task Force on Climate Preparedness and Resilience

On November 1, 2013, the President established a Task Force on Climate Preparedness and Resilience (Task Force) to advise the Administration on how to respond to the needs of communities experiencing the impacts of climate change. States, tribes and local governments across the country are already contending with more frequent or severe heat waves, droughts, wildfires, storms and floods, and other issues related to climate change. The Task Force will provide recommendations to the President on removing barriers to investments, modernizing Federal grant and loan programs to better support local efforts, and provide the information and tools needed to prepare for climate preparedness. The Task Force members include state, local, and tribal leaders from across the country who will use their experiences developing climate preparedness and resilience plans in their communities to inform their recommendations to the Administration. In December, the Task Force convened its first inaugural meeting at the White House and discussed ways to improve coordination to protect critical infrastructure, public resources, and pre-disaster preparedness. The Task Force also strategized ideas on the types of information and tools that would be most useful in confronting the impacts of climate change.

Restoring Tribal Lands

Recovering and protecting tribal land is a hallmark priority of this Administration. Secretary Jewell of the Department of the Interior set a goal of taking 500,000 acres of land into trust on behalf of Indian tribes. To date, the Administration has acquired over 195,000 acres for tribes and processed more than 1,000 separate trust applications.

Unfortunately, the efforts of the Administration to restore tribal homelands have been hampered by two recent U.S. Supreme Court decisions, *Carcieri v. Salazar* and *Match-E-Be-Nash-She-Wish Band of Pottawatomi Indians v. Patchak.* The *Carcieri* and *Patchak* decisions cast uncertainty on the Secretary of Interior's authority to acquire land in trust for tribes under the Indian Reorganization Act in some situations, and ultimately inhibit the productive use of tribal trust land. Both the *Carcieri* and *Patchak* decisions seriously undermine a primary goal of the Indian Reorganization Act, which is the acquisition of land in trust for tribes to secure a land base on which to live and engage in economic development.

Legislation has been introduced to supersede the *Carcieri* decision and to reaffirm the authority of the United States to take land into trust on behalf of Federally-recognized Indian tribes. The Administration strongly supports a legislative solution to fix the *Carcieri* decision and, to underscore that effort, the Administration included language to accomplish this in the last two Presidential budgets sent to Congress.

Last year, DOI amended the land-into-trust regulations at 25 CFR 151 to provide greater certainty to tribes in their ability to develop lands acquired in trust for purposes of housing, schools, and economic development. The final rule addresses the changes resulting from the *Patchak* case. Now, acquisition decisions made by BIA officials (at the agency or regional level), require a challenging party to seek review within the administrative appeals period. This revision creates more certainty to trust acquisitions, allowing tribes to put their newly acquired trust land to productive use as soon as possible.

Indian Land Leasing Reform

Another measure the Administration has taken to restore the authority of Indian tribes to control leasing of tribal lands is the Helping Expedite and Advance Responsible Tribal Housing (HEARTH) Act of 2012, which authorizes tribes to negotiate agricultural and business leases of tribal trust lands having a primary term of 25 years and up to two renewal terms of 25 years each, without Secretarial approval. The HEARTH Act also authorizes tribes to enter into leases for residential, recreational, religious, or educational purposes for a term up to 75 years without Secretarial approval. Prior to entering into leases, participating tribes must develop and obtain Secretarial approval of their own leasing regulations, which must include an environmental review process. To date, the Federated Indians of Graton Rancheria, the Pueblo of Sandia, the Pokagon Band of Potawatomi Indians, the Ak-Chin Indian Community, the Santa Rosa Band of Cahuilla Indians, the Citizen Potawatomi Nation, the Ewiiaapaayp Band of Kumeyaay Indians, and Kaw Nation have each received Secretarial approval of their leasing regulations. Nine additional tribes have submitted their leasing regulations to BIA for review.

Indian Trust Reform

The Administration is working to enhance tribal self-determination by initiating a comprehensive reform of Indian leasing laws and regulations. In August 2013, the Secretarial Commission on Indian Trust Administration and Reform (the Commission) held its last public meeting. The Commission was established by Secretarial Order 3292 to conduct a comprehensive evaluation of DOI's management and administration of nearly $4 billion in Indian trust assets over two years. In November 2013, the Commission presented recommendations to the Secretary of DOI. The Commission's report can be found at http://www.doi.gov/cobell/commission/index.cfm.

Self-Governance Compacts and Self-Determination Contracts

Supporting Tribal Self-Governance

The Administration strongly supports the principles of tribal self-determination and tribal self-governance and believes the Indian Self-Determination and Education Assistance Act (ISDEAA) is one of the most successful Indian policies in over 200 years. ISDEAA contracts and compacts provide the necessary flexibility for tribes to best meet the needs of their people and successfully improve tribal governmental capabilities. Because we are committed to building on what works, the Administration joins tribes once again to support recent legislation (S. 919) that will strengthen tribal control over ISDEAA contracted or compacted programs.

Contract Support Costs

At the White House Tribal Nations Conference, the President said his Administration would work to find a solution to the forward facing policy on funding Contract Support Costs (CSC). In the 2014 Appropriations bill, Congress eliminated any cap on CSC and directed the Administration to consult with tribes on a CSC long-term solution. The Administration is committed to working with tribes and Congress to fully fund Contract Support Costs within the top-line numbers set by Congressional appropriators.

Resolving Longstanding Disputes

The Administration's land settlements honorably resolve historical grievances over the accounting and mismanagement of Tribal trust funds, trust lands, and other non-monetary trust resources, which have been a source of conflict between Indian tribes and the United States.

Keepseagle Settlement

In the *Keepseagle v. Vilsack* settlement agreement, the Administration reached a $760 million settlement with Native American farmers and ranchers, who alleged discrimination by USDA's loan program. Pursuant to the agreement, the United States placed $680 million into a settlement fund and forgave nearly $60 million of outstanding Native American farm loan debt. Additionally, important programmatic relief was included in the agreement, including the establishment of a Council on Native American Farming and Ranching technical assistance to enable greater access to programs, and the publication of a program guide.

This year, USDA began reviewing applications for the Ombudsman position created by the *Keepseagle* Settlement. Furthermore, the USDA Office of Tribal Relations and the Intertribal Agriculture Council's Regional Centers increased access to USDA programs and services for Native American farmers and ranchers, resulting in Farm Service Agency loans in excess of $6 million and Natural Resource Conservation Service funding in excess of $1.75 million.

Cobell Settlement

The President signed into law the Claims Resolution Act of 2010, which authorized the *Cobell v. Salazar* settlement agreement. The settlement establishes a $1.9 billion fund for the voluntary buy-back and consolidation of fractionated land interests to address the continued proliferation of thousands of new trust accounts caused by the fractionation of land interests through succeeding generations. The land consolidation program provides individual American Indians and Alaska Natives (AI/AN) with an opportunity to obtain cash payments for divided land interests and frees up the land for the benefit of tribal communities.

Pursuant to the *Cobell* settlement terms, DOI is required to offer fair market value for purchases of fractionated interests. As such, DOI released the Land Buy-Back Program Valuation Plan on October 29, 2013, which describes how DOI determines the fair market value for land. In developing the Valuation Plan, DOI was in direct contact with multiple tribes, conducting outreach, land research, mapping, and valuation activities on reservations across Indian Country. Additionally, The Appraisal Foundation (TAF), the nation's foremost authority on appraisal standards and qualifications, performed a comprehensive review of the draft of the Valuation Plan, which was revised to incorporate all of TAF's recommendations. In December 2013, the Land Buy-Back Program completed the first land buy-back agreement with the Oglala Sioux Tribe of the Pine Ridge Reservation. Additionally, the Confederated Tribes of the Salish and Kootenai signed an agreement in January 2014.

Sustainable Economic Development

Many of the social problems that plague Native Americans arise in part from the absence of employment and economic opportunities. According to the Census Bureau, AI/AN experience poverty at 27 percent, a larger percentage than any ethnic group in the United States. Approximately 43 percent of the Native American population live in rural areas and experience many of the same challenges faced by rural America. In these places, high unemployment rates, struggling schools, distressed housing, persistent and violent crime, and health disparities cause disproportionately occurring outcomes for their residents. Native American unemployment is also 14.6 percent higher than the national average. Undoubtedly, the needs in Indian Country are great, and the Administration is redoubling its efforts to find solutions in promoting economic growth in Indian Country.

Increasing Access to Capital

Tribal leaders continue to express their frustration over access to capital and credit for business development in Indian Country. Regardless of firm size, minority-owned firms are less likely to receive loans than non-minority owned firms. While credit markets have improved, there remain gaps in loans for underserved communities.

In FY 2013, the Small Business Administration (SBA) supported nearly $100 million in lending to Native American-owned small businesses. Included in this figure is SBA's Microloan Intermediary Program. SBA Microloan Intermediary Program (loans up to $50,000) is designed for small businesses in need of small scale financing and technical assistance for startup or expansion. The loans are delivered through intermediary lenders, which are nonprofit community-based organizations with experience in lending and technical assistance. In addition to small business lending, the Microloan Program provides grants to lenders which, in turn, offers business-based training and technical assistance to micro-borrowers. SBA's Microloan Program includes a Native American-focused microloan intermediary in Wisconsin.

USDA's Farm Service Agency (FSA) also provided over $82 million in small business lending to 1,400 Native American-owned farming and ranching businesses in FY 2013. These funds were used to purchase land, equipment, and breed stock. The program assists Native American farms and ranches with their initial financing needs, providing the ability to create or enhance credit and strengthen small businesses, to improve rural economies.

Tribal Economic Development Bonds

The American Recovery and Reinvestment Act of 2009 included authority for the Department of Treasury (Treasury) to allocate $2 billion in Tribal Economic Development Bond (TEDB) authority for a wide range of projects that previously would not have qualified for tax-exempt status. The bonds interest is exempt from Federal income tax, which effectively lowers the cost of financing tribal investment projects. Due to ongoing weakness in the credit market, however, only a small amount of the originally-allocated TEDBs were issued before the initial allocations were forfeited. Currently, $1.347 billion in unused national bond authority for TEDBs remains available to tribes.

Treasury and IRS released new guidelines and application forms in 2012, to facilitate tribes' access to the remaining unused TEDB authority.[1] The new guidelines detailed the following information:

- The maximum allocation available to any one tribe is approximately $269 million (rounded) as of February 1, 2014. This per-tribe ceiling declines as the total outstanding authority is used.
- Authority is allocated immediately for approved projects, without waiting for a specific date as required by the original allocation process.
- Tribes must issue bonds within 180 days from the date of the IRS letter confirming the allocation awarded.

---

[1] For complete details see IRS Notice 2012-48 (posted at http://www.irs.gov/pub/irs-drop/n-12-48.pdf).

- IRS publishes updated Published Volume Cap Limits on the IRS website at Information for Tax Exempt Bonds (http://www.irs.gov/Tax-Exempt-Bonds).

Under current law, and apart from TEDBs, tribes have more limited authority to issue tax-exempt municipal debt than states and localities. Some tribes have challenged this policy arguing that it inhibits economic development, hampers tribes' access to the capital markets, and is unfair when compared to the broader authority granted to state and local governments.

As in prior years, the Administration's FY 2014 Revenue Proposals include key permanent changes to the structure of TEDBs. First, Treasury proposes adopting a TEDB authority eligibility standard for tribes on a permanent basis that is comparable to state or local government standards of eligibility to issue tax-exempt governmental bonds. Second, Treasury recommends adoption of a comparable private activity bond standard, with a tailored volume cap. Third, Treasury proposes project location restrictions be retained but be slightly more flexible than under current law.

Indian Loan Guaranty Insurance and Interest Subsidy Program

The Indian Loan Guaranty Insurance and Interest subsidy program ("ILGP") was established by the Indian Financing Act of 1974 to enhance economic development on Indian reservations. This program is administered by DOI's Office of Indian Energy and Economic Development (IEED). In FY 2013, the IEED made 27 loan guarantees, totaling more than $72 million. In FY 2014, IEED will be implementing a new software system that provides better information about current guarantees, the concentration of risk by industry, geographical location, and improves the ability to issue guarantees.

Community Development Financial Institutions

Treasury's Community Development Financial Institutions (CDFI) Fund administers several programs to promote access to capital and economic growth in Native American communities. Native CDFIs help create jobs, establish or improve affordable housing, and provide accessible financial services and counseling within Indian Country by increasing access to credit, capital, and financial services. The Native American CDFI Assistance (NACA) Program is funded through an annual appropriation from the United States Congress, and the awards are made each year through a competitive process that spans several months. In September 2013, Treasury announced results from the most recent round of funding for the CDFI Funds and made 35 awards totaling $12.4 million to Native organizations located in 15 states.

The CDFI Fund's Native Initiatives generate economic opportunity for Native communities by supporting the creation and expansion of Native CDFIs though the NACA Program and Capacity Building Initiative (CBI) trainings. One example of CBI training is the *The Native Leadership Journey II: Continuing Native CDFI Growth and Excellence*, a two-year comprehensive program of targeted training and technical assistance for 15 Certified Native CDFIs. Other programs include the CDFI Fund's Study on Access to Capital and Credit in Native Communities, which provides detailed analysis and quantitative research that can lead to actionable recommendations for improving access to capital and credit in Native communities and will be updated in the near future. In addition to these programs, the New Markets Tax Credit Program provides tax credits to Community Development Entities, to attract investments from the private-sector to reinvest in low-income communities.

USDA Rural Development

USDA Rural Development made significant investments in economic development projects this year by investing over $628.4 million directly benefitting AI/AN. This amount is the second highest annual investment total for Indian Country. Rural Development funds provide communities reduced financing for business loans. For example, the USDA's Intermediary Relending Program authorized $2 million in loan capital to the Confederated Tribes of the Chehalis Reservation, the Mohegan Tribe, and the Muscogee (Creek) Nation.

U.S. Department of Agriculture (USDA) Secretary Tom Vilsack (center left, second row) meets with and takes questions from the USDA Council for Native American Farming and Ranching (CNAFR) members, on Monday, Sept. 9, 2013 at the L'Enfant Plaza Hotel, in Washington, D.C. *(Department of Agriculture Photo)*

Many tribes were also recipients of value added producer grants to help develop and market corn based products, ensuring that more earnings are retained by tribal producers. These tribes include the Ute Mountain Tribe of the Ute Mountain Reservation, the Oneida Tribe of Indians of Wisconsin, and the Lower Brule Sioux Tribe of the Lower Brule Reservation. Additionally, 30 rural business enterprise grants (totaling $3.1 million) and 17 rural business opportunity grants (totaling $1.1 million) will help create and save tribal businesses and jobs throughout Indian Country.

The Federal Loan Programs for Economic and Community Development throughout Indian Country and Alaska

The President's Memorandum on Administrative Flexibility initiative led to the creation of an Interagency Working Group on Federal Loan and Credit Programs. The working group seeks to improve the deployment of Federal loan and credit programs in Indian Country by gathering information on the Federal loan programs for eligible Native American entrepreneurs and tribes.

Using this information, the working group developed a loan matrix, which informs Native Americans about relevant Federal loan programs. The matrix also includes loan and credit programs not specific to Native Americans, but broadly available to business, industry, and small business.

The Buy Indian Act

The Buy Indian Act provides the authority to set aside procurement contracts for qualified Indian-owned businesses. The final rule was published on June 7, 2013, which describes the uniform administrative procedures Federal agencies will follow to give preference for procurement of goods and services to eligible businesses that are at least 51 percent owned by one or more AI/AN individuals. The Buy Indian Act aims to increase economic activity in tribal communities and provide greater employment opportunities where Native businesses are located.

Office of Indian Energy and Economic Development (IEED)

Economic Development Feasibility Studies

Some tribal governments lack the expertise to evaluate complex business proposals. Feasibility studies empower tribal businesses to make informed decisions by distinguishing promising economic opportunities from risky investments. Since 2007, IEED has disbursed $3,730,002 in the form of 77 grants to 54 different tribes for economic development feasibility studies through its Native American Business Development Institute (NABDI).

This year, IEED grants funded feasibility studies for:

- Steam heating for residences and buildings in an Alaska Native village;
- Development of cultural tourism in an Alaska Native village;
- Retail developments for four tribes;
- Identifying businesses likely to succeed on a Great Plains reservation;
- Development of a warehouse, load-out facility, and inland port for a Minnesota tribe on land adjacent to a rail line and highway;
- Estimated profitability to export Asia baby eels caught by Native American fishermen in Maine;
- A California tribe's acquisition of a 400-acre tract of land;
- Development of a waste-to-energy plant; and
- Development of a six-to-nine megawatt hydroelectric plant.

Tribal Commercial Codes

In the last decade, significant research has been conducted to identify impediments to creating long-term sustainable economic development on Indian reservations. The Harvard Project on American Indian Economic Development found that a key factor in achieving economic self-determination is having a legal framework in place that promotes self-governance and provides a secure political environment for investors. An crucial part of this framework is a secured transactions code with a reliable lien-filing system.

IEED's Division of Economic Development and SBA joined with the Federal Reserve to sponsor training workshops for tribal governments, business managers, and tribal attorneys on how to increase creditor and investor confidence in tribal economies. The workshops emerged from a nationwide series of "Growing Economies in Indian Country" forums conducted by federal partners and the Federal Reserve Banks in 2011 to address and overcome barriers to economic development in Native American communities. Tribal commercial code workshops were held in Oklahoma City on November 13, 2012; Coushatta, Louisiana on January 15, 2013; and Albuquerque, New Mexico on February 19, 2013.

In addition, the Office of Justice Services (OJS), Bureau of Indian Affairs, and the Federal Reserve co-sponsored workshops for tribal judges and attorneys titled, "Commercial Law for the Tribal Judiciary: the Model Tribal Secured Transactions Act." These sessions focused on the scope and application of tribal secured transaction codes and issues that arise in secured transactions litigation. Training sessions took place November 29-30, 2012 in Phoenix, Arizona; January 30-31, 2013 in Seattle, Washington; March 21-22, 2013 in Oklahoma City, Oklahoma; and May 8-9, 2013 in Minneapolis, Minnesota.

Workforce Development

DOL's Trade Adjustment Assistance/Community College and Career Training Grant Competition

Trade Adjustment Assistance/Community College and Career Training (TAACCCT) grants support partnerships between community colleges and employers to develop programs that provide pathways to good jobs, including building instructional programs that meet specific industry needs. In 2013, two tribal colleges in South Dakota, applying as part of the South Dakota Allied Health Consortium, received nearly $4 million out of a $16.5 million award in the Department of Labor's (DOL) TAACCCT grant competition. This grant will enhance the health care career opportunities of tribal members and other South Dakota residents, with an emphasis on serving rural communities and reservations. Another TAACCCT award recipient was the Strengthening Workforce Alignment in Montana's Manufacturing and Energy Industries (SWAMMEI) project, which enables low-skilled student populations to access accelerated training anywhere in the state through an interactive, technology-enhanced, online curriculum. The project includes two tribal colleges, Fort Peck Community College, and Little Big Horn College.

Veteran Job Training and Promotion

DOL's Veteran Employment and Training (VETS) Office works with states to provide outreach and service delivery to qualifying Natives on or near reservations, as part of the Jobs for Veterans Act (JVA). In 2013, VETS designated a Native American Veterans Program Lead to address the needs of Native American veterans living on tribal lands. Additionally, this year the Employment and Training Administration's Division of Indian and Native American Programs (DINAP) offered technical assistance to grantees aiding Native veterans. DINAP also collaborates with VA's Office of Tribal Government Relations to further address the needs of Native veterans.

Entrepreneurial Development

Supporting American Indian and Alaska Native Businesses

According to the 2007 Census Bureau's Survey of Business Owners, there are nearly 237,000 AI/AN owned firms generating $34.4 billion in economic activity and employing over 184,000 people. MBDA funds more than 40 business centers and satellite offices, which assist minority businesses across the Nation with access to capital, contracts, and new markets. Starting last year, five new MBDA Business Centers began in states with large AI/AN populations, including: Alaska, California, New Mexico, North Dakota, and Oklahoma. These new MBDA Business Centers will receive $6.6 million over a five year period, starting in 2012.

Development Programs for Entrepreneurs

SBA District Offices and resource partners (Small Business Development Centers, Women Business Centers, SCORE, Veteran Business Outreach Centers) help 1 million entrepreneurs and small business owners each year in starting and growing their businesses by providing free or low-cost training, counseling, coaching, and mentoring. In the first three quarters of 2013 (the latest available set of data), SBA counseled and trained over 12,500 Native American small business owners. This entrepreneurial training was made possible by SBA's Office of Native American Affairs initiative, which provides support to SBA field offices throughout the United States. SBA's outreach efforts include symposiums, business development and financial literacy workshops, roundtable discussions, technical assistance, and participation in Native American conferences.

Emerging Leaders Program

The Emerging Leaders Program (formerly Emerging 200 or e200) identifies small businesses that show a high potential for growth. The program provides seven months of specialized training and resources to small businesses to build a sustainable business and promote economic development within communities historically challenged by high levels of unemployment and poverty. Sixty-two percent of participants reported increased revenues over the past year and leveraged over $26 million in new financing. Businesses also secured nearly $300 million in federal, state, local, and tribal contracts. The 2013 Emerging Leaders training cycle included over 40 Native American owned small businesses enrolled in markets across the country.

The Native Communities Entrepreneurial Empowerment Outreach Training

SBA's Native Communities Entrepreneurial Empowerment Outreach training reached rural reservations this year, thereby enhancing the capacity of organizations to serve Native American business communities. SBA's empowerment outreach was charged with addressing four priorities: (1) increasing knowledge; (2) expanding the capacity and overall development of hosting organizations; (3) strengthening existing and new relationships throughout Indian Country; and (4) increasing knowledge of entrepreneurship programs, and growing the capacity of Native-owned businesses. Over 400 participants received small business development training at 23 events that extended across sixteen states. Participants estimated they would create 499 full-time jobs and 205 part-time jobs throughout the country over the next year.

Procurement and Marketing Training Conferences

One of the quickest means of spurring job growth in Native communities is to expand operations and increase revenues for tribal businesses through government and private sector procurement contracts. IEED has worked with the U.S. Department of Defense's (DOD) Native American Procurement Technical Assistance Centers (PTACs) and tribal organizations to host one-on-one business development sessions to bring together tribal businesses potential government buyers. Over the past several years, IEED has partnered with PTACs to sponsor regional matchmaking events in Texas, Nevada, Montana, Minnesota, California, Alaska, Washington, Virginia, and North Dakota. Nearly 600 Native American businesses and 100 corporate and government buyers participated in these events. These events build deeper personal relationships between Native businesses and potential government and commercial customers. Over time, these relationships lead to new contracts for Native businesses and more jobs for Native communities.

IEED also participated in the Affiliated Tribes of Northwest Indians (ATNI) 60th Annual Convention, hosted by the Coeur d'Alene Tribe in Worley, Idaho on September 15-19, 2013. The Convention encouraged the purchase of Native-produced foods by prime contractors, tribal casinos, and restaurants. Thirty-two representatives from tribes with casinos and restaurants interested in purchasing Native food products were matched with nine Native food producers, all of which were prequalified to meet the capability standards of large food distributors. IEED orchestrated marketing presentations by each of the Native food producers and organized one-on-one matchmaking sessions between producers and potential buyers.

Supporting Infrastructure Development in Indian Country

Essential Tribal Facilities

USDA Rural Development invested $114.7 million in FY 2013 to help finance essential tribal community facilities, through its Community Facilities Program. Also this year, the largest single investment to a tribe in the program's history was made to the Mississippi Band of Choctaw Indians ($40 million direct loan and $10 million loan guarantee) to help the Tribe finance a state-of-the-art health care facility. In addition, 24 grants ($3 million) were provided to Tribal Colleges and Universities.

Land Acquisition

In 2013, the Forest Service's Community Forest Program implemented the first-ever lands purchasing grant for which tribes are eligible. The program provides financial assistance to local governments, tribal governments, and qualified nonprofit entities to protect forests that provide continuing and accessible community benefits. The Eastern Band of Cherokee received the first grant under this program, which enabled them to purchase culturally important lands at Hall Mountain.

Housing

Loans for Native American Homeowners

Historically, Native Americans have had limited access to private mortgage capital, primarily because of the lending community's lack of familiarity with collateralizing loans on trust land. Several government agencies work to educate the lending community, especially agencies like the Department of Housing and Urban Development's (HUD). HUD's loan guarantee program encourages private lenders to invest in Indian Country. In FY 2013, 61 Native Hawaiian families and 3,852 AI/AN families obtained mortgage financing with assistance from these programs. Notably, the foreclosure rate consistently remains low, at only 2.5 percent in November 2013.

USDA Rural Development loans and grants also provide much needed financing for the purchase and repair of single-family homes. This year, AI/ANs were eligible to receive housing grants through Single Family Housing direct loans ($19 million) and Single Family Housing loan guarantees ($155 million). USDA Rural Development also provided $1.3 million in grants to very low income AI/AN homeowners to help make much needed repairs and improvements to their homes

Additionally, VA Loan Guaranty Service continues to work with Federally-recognized tribes to provide direct home loans to veterans through the Native American Veteran Direct Loan Program (NADL). VA's Loan Guaranty Service reported 951 loans granted and over 85 participating tribes in FY 2013. Loan Guaranty Service personnel participate in tribal town hall sessions and conduct outreach to tribal representatives to ensure access to their programs for veterans among participating tribes. The loan guaranty service continue to work with nonparticipating tribes to see if they are amenable to permitting VA to offer home financing to eligible veterans.

Indian Housing Block Grant Programs

In FY 2013, HUD's Indian Community Block Grant program awarded more than $53.6 million to 76 tribes or tribal organizations around the country to develop sustainable Native American communities, including the creation of housing, suitable living environments, and economic opportunities for low and moderate income households. Most of the funds awarded in 2013 were used to rehabilitate substandard housing and build new and affordable housing.

The President's FY 2014 Budget Request includes $650 million for the Indian Housing Block Grant, which is to date the largest single source of funds for housing assistance in Indian Country. HUD expects to award these funds to approximately 366 recipients representing more than 553 tribes in 34 states. The amount requested will support a wide range of housing assistance activities, including the construction, acquisition, or substantial rehabilitation of approximately 5,800 affordable homes. In addition, the grants will fund the modernization and maintenance of approximately 50,000 housing units that were developed prior to the enactment of the Native American Housing Assistance and Self-Determination Act of 1996 (NAHASDA).

Native American Housing Needs Assessments

From 2010 to 2012, HUD held regional and national outreach meetings with tribal leaders and tribal housing stakeholders to seek tribal input on Native American housing needs. The outreach plan and survey instruments were refined based on input from these sessions and comments from the expert panel formulated specifically for the study. In spring 2013, HUD conducted a pilot of the household survey, and the survey is expanding to include to 40 randomly selected tribes. An interim report was published in November 2013, and is available on HUD's website. The final report is scheduled for publication in fall 2014.

Transportation

Tribal Transportation Program Agreements

Over the past two years, BIA has developed a new program agreement created by the Division of Transportation and the Department of Interior to substantially decrease the amount of time it takes for tribal transportation funds distribution to tribes. Over 160 tribes have chosen to enter into Tribal Transportation Program Agreements. As a result, tribes have greater flexibility under the law to prioritize where and when transportation funds should be expended. In addition, more than 85 tribal governments and consortiums (totaling 120 Tribes) operate their transportation programs directly through The Federal Highway Administration (FHWA) under a similar program agreement. In 2013, the Tribal FHWA Program Agreements transferred more than $133 million of the Tribal Transportation Program funding to tribes.

MAP-21

The Department of Transportation (DOT) also supports the development of critical transportation infrastructure in Indian Country through various programs and services. On July 6, 2012, President Obama signed the Moving Ahead for Progress in the 21st Century Act (MAP-21). Under MAP-21, the Indian Reservation Roads Program was redesigned and renamed the Tribal Transportation Program (TTP), authorized at $450 million per year, with a new formula program to distribute funds to Federally-recognized tribes.

MAP-21 provides $30 million to the Federal Transit Administration's (FTA) TTP – $25 million to the formula program and $5 million to the discretionary program. Discretionary funds are made available annually on a competitive basis. Eligible activities under both programs include capital, planning, and operating assistance. To implement the program, FTA's consultation included two face-to-face meetings held in November and December 2012 with Indian tribes and other interested stakeholders, and a notice and comment period through a public docket which was open from November 2012 until January 2013 to receive comments on proposed implementation strategies. Over 150 individuals attended the consultation sessions, and more than 25 tribes commented to the public docket. Comments ranged from the eligibility of projects to concerns with illustrative formula apportionments.

Additionally, FTA is in the process of revising the Formula Grants for Rural Areas (Section 5311) Circular to include a chapter that will provide guidance to tribes receiving TTP funds. The proposed circular was open for public comment until November 25, 2013. FTA hosted a webinar on November 7, 2013 to highlight the changes made to the proposed guidance for the Section 5311 Program. FTA also conducted three Tribal Transit workshops in November and December of 2013 with Indian tribes. The workshops included updates on MAP-21 and provided technical assistance to the tribes.

DOT also continues to support highway safety in Indian Country through the development and implementation of a national tribal safety plan and by providing technical assistance to several tribal governments nationwide. Safety summits have identified tribal safety priorities and strengthened partnerships to address safety challenges. Safety plans were developed with tribal leadership in places including the Ft. Berthold Indian Reservation in North Dakota where a dramatic increase in truck traffic has impacted the local community. The new legislation provides an additional set-aside of TTP funds for highway safety projects. FHWA received more than 240 tribal applications for these funds, and Secretary Foxx of the Department of Transportation announced at the White House Tribal Nations Conference that awards would be made to more than 180 of the applicants. MAP-21 also continues the Indian Highway Safety Program and authorizes funding at $4.7 million. DOT will be working with tribes during the implementation process to provide training and technical assistance. Twenty-eight tribes have already been awarded grants for FY 2014 under the Indian Highway Safety Program.

MAP-21 also provides funding to improve bridges and in FY 2013, FHWA awarded $8.6 million to tribes for 18 bridge improvement projects.

Finally, FHWA continues to work through the Tribal Transportation Program Coordinating Committee, (formerly the Indian Reservation Roads Program Coordinating Committee) to develop draft guidance on how to make funding available directly for tribes to address planning, law enforcement, education, and engineering safety issues in Indian Country. FHWA partnered with BIA to update regulations required by MAP-21 and convened multiple listening sessions with tribes across the country.

High-Speed Wireless Internet

National Telecommunications & Information Administration

The Administration is working with tribal leaders to bring Indian communities into the 21st Century by equipping them with high speed access to the internet. The Recovery Act allocated approximately $4 billion to the National Telecommunications and Information Administration (NTIA) for the Broadband Technology Opportunities Program (BTOP). BTOP was responsible for funding grants that increased broadband access and adoption in underserved communities nationwide. Indian tribes received approximately 27 percent of the funding for 56 projects.

The Pyramid Lake Paiute Tribe received a seven million dollar BTOP grant to fund a fiber optic network, "Natukwena Nagwesenoo," which in the Paiute language means "to weave information." This project is bringing access to high-speed broadband to key community anchor institutions on the reservation, including educational institutions for children and adults, regional health services, and community centers. NTIA also awarded $1.6 million to the Nez Perce Tribe, which is now providing wireless broadband service to homes in three counties. Lastly, the Ute Tribe received a $1.5 million grant and completed installation of a fiber optic backbone that offers broadband wireless service for social service agencies, police stations, and homes on the Unitah and Ouray Reservations.

In 2013, USDA's Rural Utilities Service (RUS) provided funding to tribal entities that received awards under the Broadband Initiatives Program (BIP). These funds were used to construct facilities that provide high speed broadband service to a number of tribal communities throughout the country. Also, under the Broadband Loan Program, RUS approved a loan to Northeast Rural Services, Inc. (NRS) to provide broadband service to a number of underserved areas in Oklahoma. NRS' rural service area population includes members of nine Native American Tribes with the Cherokee Nation having members throughout the entire service area.

Water

DOI continues to work to resolve Indian water rights claims as part of the Administration's commitment to bring water to tribal communities and enhance economic development on reservations. This year was marked with several major milestones in Indian water rights. DOI executed the Aamodt Final Settlement Agreement and related agreements and waivers in accordance with the 2010 Aamodt water settlement legislation. DOI also finalized the execution of the White Mountain Apache Water Rights Quantification documents, the final of the four settlements under the Claims Resolution Act. BIA and the Bureau of Reclamation will work to implement these settlements.

DOI is moving forward with implementation of the newly enacted water settlements and continuing progress on existing settlements. In 2013, the Bureau of Reclamation provided more than $1.7 million in funding to Pueblos in New Mexico through several programs such as the Native American Program, the Pueblo Irrigation Infrastructure Program, the Water Conservation Program, and the Middle Rio Grande Project for projects and studies related to drought and wildfires.

The Bureau of Reclamation continues to fund and construct the Navajo-Gallup Water Supply Project which was included in the Navajo Nation Water Rights Settlement Agreement. This project is designed to provide a long-term sustainable water supply to serve Natives in the eastern portion of the Navajo Reservation, the southwestern portion of the Jicarilla Apache Reservation, and the city of Gallup, New Mexico. Construction of this project is scheduled for completion in 2024.

Finally, USDA's Office of Rural Development invested $45.7 million in water and environmental projects benefitting tribal communities throughout FY 2013. This amount includes $22.5 million invested in 48 states and an additional $23.2 million benefitting tribal communities in Alaska, much of which was provided through the Rural Alaska Village Grants program.

Energy Development

The Administration continues to implement an all-of-the-above strategy to expand domestic energy production in Indian Country. Indian Trust lands are rich in natural resources, but they also are home to some of the poorest communities in the United States. As such, tribal lands hold great renewable energy potential, and smart development of these resources can strengthen tribal economies, create jobs, and generate clean electricity for communities.

IEED's Division of Energy and Mineral Development believes that development of energy resources should be used as a springboard for development that will positively affect the local economy. Energy and mineral resource development is the largest revenue generator in Indian Country, with projected future royalty income climbing to one billion dollars per year. The following chart provides additional information about the significant impact energy and mineral development has on reservation economies.

Commodity	Value ($ billions)	% of Total Value	Estimated Economic Impact ($ billions)	% of Total Economic Impact	Estimated Jobs Impact (jobs)	% of Total Estimated Jobs Impact
Oil, Gas, Coal	3.31	80.9	9.63	79.7	96,080	76.4
Minerals	.3	7.3	.86	7.1	15,434	12.3
Subtotal	**3.61**	**88.2**	**10.49**	**86.8**	**111,514**	**88.7**
Irrigation	.39		.95		8,791	
Timber	.04		.56		4,069	
Grazing	.04		.08		1,370	
Total	**4.09**		**12.08**		**125,744**	

Source: Table modified from *The Department of the Interior's Economic Contributions – July 9, 2012* Chapter 2 – Bureau-Level Economic Contributions

BIA is involved in 50 renewable energy projects with 40 different tribal entities on projects including biomass, waste to energy, geothermal, hydroelectric, solar, and wind resources. In 2013, IEED's Division of Energy and Mineral Development (DEMD) estimated Indian royalties to be approximately $900 million, and within two years estimates a total over $1 billion.

Renewable Energy Development

Strategic Technical Assistance Response Team Program

The Department of Energy's (DOE) Office of Indian Energy is primarily responsible for directing, coordinating, and implementing energy planning, education, management, and programs that assist tribes with energy development, capacity building, development of energy infrastructure, reduction of energy costs, and the electrification of Indian lands and homes. In FY 2013, the DOE Office of Indian Energy invested over $1.8 million in new technical assistance, education, and capacity building programs to support tribes in developing clean energy resources. These programs included the Strategic Technical Assistance Response Team (START) Program, education and training for project development and project finance, tribal leader forums on energy development issues, transmission analysis and support, and other hands-on technical assistance on tribal projects.

The START Program was designed by DOE's Office of Indian Energy to help tribes move from feasibility to real development of clean energy projects. START empowers tribal leaders to tap into their clean energy resources by offering the tools and on-the-ground resources needed to lead strategic energy projects that can foster energy self-sufficiency, sustainability, and economic competitiveness. Specifically, the START Program works directly with tribal communities to evaluate project financial and technical feasibility, provide on-going training to community members, and help implement a variety of clean energy projects, including energy storage infrastructure, renewable energy deployment, and energy efficiency. DOE continues to meet directly with tribal governments and energy enterprise leaders, to discuss updates on the cutting edge START projects.

Organized Village of Kake, Alaska

One of the five initial Alaska START projects, the Organized Village of Kake, was particularly successful in reaping the benefits of START assistance. A START-led strategic energy planning workshop brought together Kake's tribal government and local stakeholders to incorporate stakeholder and community member involvement to help Alaska Native villages take advantage of their local renewable resources to reduce their dependency on high cost diesel and heating oil. Accordingly, the START Program relocated a wind met-tower closer to the village's transmission lines, which provided a lower-cost transmission option for wind energy development. DOE also helped the Tribe install a 5.8-kW solar photovoltaic (PV) system. Together, these initiatives helped Kake reduce diesel fuel demand and provided alternative energy sources through clean energy projects. Based on the success of the initial Alaska START projects, five more Alaska Native villages were selected in 2013, including: the Native Village of Kongiganak, Native Village of Koyukuk, Native Village of Minto, Native Village of Shishmaref, and Yakutat T'lingit Tribe.

Passamaquoddy Tribes of Indian Township and Pleasant Point in Maine

Passamaquoddy Tribes of Indian Township and Pleasant Point in Maine were also initial recipients of START Assistance. The tribes requested help with developing a commercial-scale wind farm to generate revenue. START validated existing wind resource data and siting for the project and trained tribal leaders and project teams on the New Markets Tax Credit Program. The START Program also led a strategic energy planning workshop that brought both communities together to identify and overcome challenges, refine shared vision for renewable energy development, and determine next steps to help better position the tribes to make informed procurement and ownership decisions regarding the proposed wind development. Five projects were selected for the second START Renewable Energy Project Development Program in 2013, which focuses on community-scale clean energy projects, including: Chugachmiut Regional Corporation, Ho-Chunk Nation, Pinoleville Pomo Nation, San Carlos Apache Tribe, and Southern Ute Indian Tribe.

Moapa Energy Development

In June 2012, DOI approved a 350-megawatt solar energy project on the Moapa River Indian Reservation in Clark County, Nevada. The Moapa Paiute tribe set aside 2,000 acres of their 72,000 Reservation for energy development. The project is financed by the Los Angeles City Council, which approved a 25 year purchase agreement with K Road Moapa Solar, LLC for up to 250 megawatts of power. Notably, the project is the first-ever, utility scale solar project approved for development on tribal lands.

Due to the overwhelming success of the first Moapa Solar Project, the tribe is working with RES Americas to propose a second project called the Moapa Solar Energy Project. The proposed project involves constructing and operating a solar energy generation center that would generate 230,000-290,000 Megawatt Hours per year. The Moapa Solar Energy Center Project would be located on tribal lands held in trust for the Moapa Band. DOI issued a Notice of Intent to prepare an Environmental Impact Statement for the project on August 6, 2012. The Record of Decision is targeted for 2014.

Division of Energy and Mineral Development

IEED, through its DEMD office, has worked to expand tribal energy development and create jobs and economic growth in tribal communities. IEED experienced growing tribal interest this year in community-based biomass projects, ranging from 250 kW to 5 MW. DEMD is actively engaged in renewable energy development in Indian Country through its Energy and Mineral Development Program (EMDP) and its on-going technical assistance efforts. DEMD provides grant funding to help tribal entities conduct resource assessments, feasibility studies, and business planning activities related to their renewable energy development objectives.

At the close of FY2013, DEMD was involved in 50 renewable energy projects with 41 different tribal entities. These development projects include:

- The Fond Du Lac Band developed a market for heating with wood biomass (chip and pellet) as opposed to costly propane and fuel oil. The Band utilized DEMD technical assistance as well as feasibility funding.
- The Confederated Salish and Kootenai Tribe on the Flathead Reservation are scheduled to acquire the Kerr Dam hydroelectric facility beginning in September of 2015. DEMD is providing technical assistance and funding to help the Tribe prepare for the acquisition.

- The Crow Nation in Montana has utilized the DEMD staff and feasibility funding to assess the Yellowtail Afterbay Dam for hydroelectric energy.
- The Cherokee Nation has utilized DEMD staff and funding to confirm the feasibility of installing a 33 MW hydroelectric power plant on the Mayo Dam.
- The Cherokee Nation, Pawnee, Otoe Missouria, Kaw, and Ponca Tribes are pursuing the development of a wind project on the Chilocco School site in Oklahoma. DEMD is assisting the through technical assistance and feasibility funding.
- DEMD is involved in the development of hydroelectric turbine installation on four dams along the Truckee River on the Pyramid Lake Reservation.

This year, USDA Rural Development's Electric Programs also invested $275.3 million in bringing new and improved electric infrastructure to AI/AN from coast to coast. The total includes a $167 million loan to the Navajo Tribal Utility Authority headquartered in Fort Defiance, Arizona.

Geothermal Energy Development

DEMD is providing financial and technical assistance to tribes through Energy and Mineral Development Grants with potential for commercial electrical generation. The program has successfully drilled a low temperature geothermal well to be utilized for space heating at the White River Indian Health Center on the Rosebud Reservation in South Dakota. DEMD is also involved in discoveries on two separate reservations with high temperature resource areas with potential for commercial electrical generation. One reservation is the Pauite-Shoshone Tribe of the Fallon Reservation in Nevada, whereby DEMD funded studies for drilling shallow temperature gradient holes after seismic evaluation. Similarly, DEMD funded studies at the Pyramid Lake Reservation, which resulted in the discovery of a very high temperature gradient on the northeast border of the Reservation.

Conventional Energy Development

Developing Oil and Gas Energy Resources

DOI's IEED helps spur job creation and economic activity on reservations by assisting tribes in developing energy and mineral resources. This year, IEED assisted Indian mineral owners in the negotiation of seven Indian Mineral Development Act (IMDA) agreements for oil and natural gas development. These leases have the potential to produce over $20 billion in revenue to the Indian mineral owner over the life of the lease, through both royalties and working interests. IEED staff offers a unique, hands-on approach to assisting tribes in leasing their oil and gas resources. By keeping tribes well informed, IEED is able to adjust transaction terms such as royalty rates, lease bonuses, and term of lease, to ensure that both the tribe and its potential partner operate from the same base of information. Moreover, they also include rigorous work commitments as part of the negotiated agreement, which results in the development of Indian land. This kind of technical assistance during negotiations between tribes and potential partners has resulted in tribes achieving a nationwide average Indian oil royalty rate of 16.88 percent, far in excess of the nationwide federal lands (BLM lands) oil royalty rate of 11.29 percent.

In March 2012, the U.S. Department of Commerce's Economic Development Administration (EDA) awarded $1 million to the Fort Peck Assiniboine & Sioux Tribes of Montana to help expand the Tribe's oil drilling services operations. EDA's investment funds the renovation and expansion of an existing building and the purchase of specialized equipment for the development of a tribally-owned pipe rethreading operation at Fort Peck Tech Services. As a result, the Tribe's entrance into the oilfield services industry is creating new high-wage, higher-skilled jobs that can be sustained for decades. Native Americans average an Indian oil royalty rate of 16.88 percent, which is far greater than the nationwide federal oil royalty rate of 11.29 percent.

Coal Development & Mine Safety on Indian Lands

DEMD has worked with the Crow Tribe since 2005 to better understand both the quality and quantity of coal in a proposed lease area on the Crow Reservation. These resource calculations provided critical information that laid the ground work for negotiating the terms of two subsequent leasing agreements. The resulting deals will yield a cash flow of approximately $11 billion and generate $14 to $21 million in total salaries per year.

Despite efforts to develop coal resources, extreme physical hazards are common at abandoned mine sites. Beginning in 2010, the Office of Surface and Mining Reclamation Enforcement (OSM), in close coordination with the Cherokee Nation government, investigated, designed, and awarded reclamation contracts for two separate Abandoned Mine Land (AML) initiatives: the Dwight Mission and Cherokee West AML Reclamation Projects. Work began in September 2013 on the Dwight Mission Project under a $1.79 million contract to eliminate safety hazards and create a 25-acre recreational lake. Additionally, the work is nearly complete on the Cherokee West AML Reclamation Project in the Porum Recreation Area. The $370,000 contract eliminates serious public safety hazards, creates safe access to an existing recreational lake, and improves the habitat and recreational values of the reclaimed tribal lands.

Fort Berthold Energy Development

In 2013, DEMD provided technical services and financial support to the Fort Berthold Indian Reservation, in order to support shale oil and gas development that is occurring in western North Dakota. At the Fort Berthold Indian Reservation, oil and gas has been the largest driver of economic development. The level of drilling activity continues to increase from 150 wells drilled through the end of 2010 to 400 additional wells drilled in 2011 and 2012. That represents a doubling of work load that is expected to continue through 2013, with development rates leveling off to 100 wells per year over the next 5 years. It is expected that 1,000 wells will be drilled to initially develop the Bakken Formation and an additional 1,000 wells to complete full development of the Bakken and Three Forks Formations over the next 10 to 20 years.

Increased Level of Support to Tribes and Individual Indian Mineral Owners

Indian tribes and BIA are challenged by the growing demand for leasing, permitting, and drilling in Indian Country. In light of these increasing demands, BIA and DEMD put a team of technical staff at the Fort Berthold Indian Reservation to provide on-site services. This team included realty specialists, environmental specialists, and petroleum engineers. DEMD also provided geographic information system data (GIS) and data management support through the implementation of the National Indian Oil and Gas Management System (NIOGEMS) to ensure proper communication and coordination occur between the various departmental agencies, affiliated tribes, and individual Indian mineral owners.

A similar scenario is beginning to occur on several other reservations, potentially creating backlogs for the issuance of leases and permits. These tribes are affected by increasing demands for leases and permits, including the Uintah and Ouray Reservation (Northern Ute Tribe), Navajo, Osage Tribe, Blackfeet Tribe, and Jicarilla Apache Tribe. BIA and DEMD are acting quickly to prevent future delays in drilling wells by providing additional support staff at several of the Agencies and technical support.

Supporting Access to Greater Nutrition and Healthcare

Health disparities continue to persist between Native Americans and other racial and ethnic groups. The Administration has placed a renewed focus on ending these health disparities by improving the health and well-being of tribal communities, expanding access to preventive care and reducing chronic disease, and focusing on childhood obesity.

The Affordable Care Act and Implementation of the Indian Health Care Improvement Act

The President achieved historic gains in health security for every American family through the passage of the Affordable Care Act (ACA), which included the permanent reauthorization of the Indian Health Care Improvement Act (IHCIA). The ACA also includes special provisions for Native Americans related to the implementation of the Health Insurance Marketplace that will allow enrollees to purchase affordable health insurance or participate in the planned Medicaid expansion in 2014.

Starting in 2014, ACA requires each individual to have minimum essential health coverage or be required to make a shared responsibility payment when filing his or her federal income tax return. On June 26, Centers for Medicare & Medicaid Services (CMS) issued a final rule allowing all AI/ANs who are eligible to receive services from an Indian healthcare provider to apply for and receive an exemption from the shared responsibility payment if they do not maintain minimum essential coverage under the ACA. This rule was a direct result of consultation and input from tribes on the issue of the definitions of "Indian" in the ACA that conflicted with such eligibility. This exemption is in addition to the pre-existing exemption in the law for AI/AN members of Federally-recognized tribes.

The ACA also provides a new health insurance option for tribal employers to allow tribes or tribal organizations that are operating programs under the Indian Self-Determination and Education Assistance Act or Urban Indian organizations carrying out programs under Title 5 of the IHCIA, to enroll their employees and families in the Federal Employees Health Benefits (FEHB) Program. The Office of Personnel Management (OPM) is implementing this new health insurance option for tribal employers. Since May 2012, 55 tribal employers in 15 States have enrolled approximately 10,000 individuals in FEHB.

The ACA supports the Maternal, Infant, and Early Childhood Home Visiting (MIECHV) program, administered by the Administration for Children and Families (ACF) and Health

Resources and Services Administration (HRSA). These programs allow states, tribes (through a 3 percent set-aside), and territories to deliver services for early childhood home visitation programs, and provide comprehensive services to improve outcomes for families living in at-risk communities. ACF also awarded five grants to tribal organizations through the Health Profession Opportunity Grants (HPOG) Program, which provides education and training to TANF recipients and other low-income individuals for high paying and high demand health care occupations.

IHS continues to provide cooperative agreements for national tribal organizations to develop and disseminate consumer-oriented materials in order to help AI/ANs understand their rights under the ACA. The National Indian Health Outreach and Education (NIHOE) organizations developed a website to provide consumer-oriented education materials and training tools for community representatives at www.tribalhealthcare.org. The website provides basic information about the ACA as it relates to the Indian health care system and resources for individual consumers, health directors, tribal employees, and tribal governments. As of 2013, the NIHOE grantees have conducted over 350 ACA trainings for Tribal communities.

Providing Greater Access to Care

Contract Health Service Program

IHS continues to strengthen federal efforts to improve the quality of and access to Indian health care through its internal reform efforts and key collaborations with other Federal entities. IHS continues to focus on its priority to improve the quality of and access to care with a continued emphasis on customer service and several quality improvement strategies including the establishment of a patient centered medical home model within the Indian health system. IHS, in collaboration with Indian Tribes, implemented key tribal recommendations to improve business practices in the Contract Health Service (CHS) program. CHS's online curriculum model is already implemented in 127 of the IHS, Tribal, and Urban Indian health programs and has reduced wait times, provided better coordination and continuity of care, and allowed quicker scheduling of appointments.

National Health Service Corps Program

The National Health Service Corps (NHSC) program designates which health sites in the Indian health care system are eligible for the recruitment and retention of healthcare providers. The NHSC Virtual Job Fair for Tribal Sites in March 2013 focused on helping NHSC approved IHS health clinics and tribal clinics to advertise more than 100 open vacancies. In addition, the job fair featured 23 "virtual recruitment" presentations by IHS, as well as tribal health care delivery sites from 8 states, representing more than 32 individual sites. The July and August NHSC Virtual Job Fairs for Tribal Sites helped NHSC Scholars find jobs at high-need sites and offered 9 presentations representing more than 95 tribal health care delivery sites and 67 job vacancies. n November 2013, the NHSC Virtual Job Fair provided 36 NHSC sites from 21 states and the District of Columbia the opportunity to promote 150 primary care medical, dental, mental, and behavioral health job openings to a targeted audience of primary care job seekers. 5 of the participating NHSC sites were tribal, representing at least 11 job vacancies in underserved areas. Additional NHSC Virtual Job Fairs are planned throughout 2014.

NHSC also provides a free on-line recruitment resource where all NHSC-approved sites can post job positions connecting tribal sites to primary care professionals seeking employment throughout the country. As of October 2013, more than 6,050 NHSC sites had a Jobs Center profile, and thousands of primary care professionals access the site each month.

As a result of these collaborations, the number of NHSC-approved placement Indian health program sites rose from 588 to 622 for the year ending November 2013. This compares to 494 such sites approved in 2011 and 60 in 2010. Between November 2012 and November 2013, the number of primary care medical, dental, and behavioral and mental health care providers rose from 344 to 372.

Health Resources and Services Administration

HRSA's community health center program grantees served over 260,000 AI/ANs in calendar year 2012. Approximately $45 million was awarded to dually funded health centers in FY 2012 and nearly $40 million was awarded in FY 2013. In 2011, HRSA began a Teaching Health Center Graduate in Medical Education (THCGME) program, which allocates $230 million for health centers in Native American communities. The purpose of the program is to increase the number of primary care residents and dentists trained in community-based ambulatory patient care settings. The program is administered by the Bureau of Health Professions and authorized and funded by the Affordable Care Act.

One standout from the THCGME program is The Puyallup Tribal Health Authority (PTHA), which began receiving funding in FY 2012. Outpatient training occurs at the PTHA's Takopid Health Center, a tribal-operated clinic within IHS, on the Puyallup Indian Reservation. The Takopid Health Center provides ambulatory care for an annual total of 96,000 primary care medical visits for 9,000 patients. Residents receive training with an emphasis on cultural awareness and develop a keen understanding of how Native American culture impacts clinical service.

Certified Electronic Health Record Technology

IHS continues to actively support the Administration's initiative promoting meaningful use of Certified Electronic Health Record Technology. Through the end of FY 2013, eligible hospitals and providers across the Indian health care system earned $88 million in Medicare and Medicaid Electronic Health Record (EHR) Incentive Programs payments. IHS continues to work closely with the National Indian Health Board Regional Extension Center to promote meaningful use among providers. This year, IHS has been preparing for 2014 Certification, which will allow eligible hospitals and providers to continue to participate in the Medicare and Medicaid EHR Incentive Programs.

VA/IHS National Reimbursement Agreement

The VA/IHS National Agreement covers all IHS Federal healthcare facilities nationwide, and allows VA to reimburse IHS for direct care services provided to eligible AI/AN veterans. This year, VA and IHS made substantial progress by completing the implementation of the Agreement in all 10 federal pilot sites and making progress on its implementation in all other IHS Federal facilities. During implementation, VA and IHS completed ten Phase I Pilot Sites two months ahead of schedule in March 2013 and were able to finalize all remaining 71 local implementation plans in July 2013.

IHS Hospital Consortium, in collaboration with the Centers for Medicare & Medicaid Services, established the Partnership for Patients (PfP) quality initiative in IHS operated hospitals, to reduce both hospital acquired conditions (HACs) and hospital readmission rates. The Consortium establishes measures for all HACs and readmissions, increasing the frequency at which hospitals are providing PfP data and showing improvement trends for services available within each respective hospital. The 2014 PfP improvement goals include a further reduction of readmission rates by at least 20 percent. In an effort to achieve this goal, IHS Hospital Consortium has engaged Econometrica Inc., a research and management organization committed to providing cost-effective analyses, modeling, and economic evaluations to work with each hospital. IHS Hospital Consortium will work with IHS hospitals to attain and maintain Medicare hospital quality standards to improve patient safety.

In FY 2013, IHS increased access to health care by improving eight IHS health care facilities that provide healthcare to over 65,000 AI/ANs. These facilities include the Arapahoe Health Center, the Copper River Native Association Joint Venture facility, the Barrow Hospital, the Fairbanks Chief Isaac Health Center Joint Venture facility, the Kenai Dena'ina Health Clinic Joint Venture facility, the Tishomingo Chickasaw Health Center Joint Venture facility, the Nome Hospital, and the Alaska Native Medical Center renovations. They each achieved targets on all Government Performance and Results Act clinical indicators, which measure the quality of care delivered in IHS, Tribal, and urban Indian health programs. Significant improvements have also been demonstrated in the completion of tobacco cessation education, depression screenings, receipt of mammograms, screening for cardiovascular disease, and receipt of screenings for colonoscopies.

The Veterans Health Administration (VHA) Office of Rural Health (ORH) promotes collaborations with tribal entities to increase access to transportation, outreach, primary care, mental health care, education, and specialty care services for rural AI/AN veterans. ORH funded 16 AI/AN focused initiatives, investing nearly $6 million in FY 2013. ORH's Veterans Rural Health Resource Center-Western Region (VRHRC-WR) is piloting multiple projects to improve health care outcomes for AI/AN Veterans. One project established a Native Veteran Telehealth Collaborative Education and Consultation Service to expand collaborative VA Telemental Health Services for rural Native veterans. OHR also funded the Alaska Rural Telebehavioral Health project in collaboration with the Southeast Alaska Regional Health Consortium, which increases access to VHA mental health care for veterans in the Sitka area and provides services to 18 Native Alaskan communities. In addition, ORH supports telehealth initiatives serving Native veterans living in rural Montana, Wyoming, North Dakota, and South Dakota, including the Pine Ridge and Standing Rock Indian Reservations.

Addressing Health Disparities

The Affordable Care Act

While the overall health of the nation has improved over time, striking health disparities continue to exist between AI/AN and other racial and ethnic groups. A recent report by the Institute of Medicine found that inadequate data on race, ethnicity, and language barriers lowers the likelihood of effective actions to address health disparities. The ACA puts a renewed focus on efforts to eliminate disparities that AI/AN currently face in health, including investments in data collection and research about those health disparities. Now, any Federally-conducted or supported health program, activity, or survey must collect and report data on race, ethnicity, sex, geographic area, primary language, and disability status.

ACA also codifies into law the Office of Minority Health (OMH) within HHS and a network of minority health offices to monitor healthcare trends and quality of care among minority patients at the state and federal levels and to also evaluate the success of minority health programs and initiatives. Finally, ACA elevates the National Center for Minority Health and Health Disparities at the National Institutes of Health from a Center to a full Institute, adding to the nation's capacity to address health disparities for minorities.

Office of Minority Health

The Office of Minority Health's AI/AN Health Disparities Program is designed to strengthen the capacity of Tribal Epidemiology Centers (TECs) and Urban Indian Health Programs (UIHPs) to collect and manage data more effectively, better understand and develop the link between public health problems and behavior, socioeconomic conditions, and geography, and create a pipeline program for students to increase racial and ethnic diversity in the public health and biomedical sciences professions. OMH awarded competitive funding in FY 2012 for a project period of five years (FY 2012 – FY 2017) to six TECs to carry out disease surveillance. In addition to building data capacity, TECs and UHIPs are required to form collaborative partnerships to improve access to quality health and human services, and design programs to increase the number of American Indian and Alaska Natives serving as health professionals, para-professionals, and researchers. The Office of Minority Health Resource Center (OMHRC) has developed a Native-focused HIV curriculum called the Circle of Life. This internet-based curriculum focuses on middle school students.

Reducing Diabetes and Heart Disease

IHS, in partnership with tribes, continues to implement successful efforts to reduce diabetes and cardiovascular disease risk factors in AI/AN people with innovative and culturally appropriate activities. The Administration supported a one year extension of the Special Diabetes Program for Indians (SDPI) through 2014 to help prevent and treat diabetes and its complications. The Tribal Leaders Diabetes Committee (TLDC) met with IHS in December 2012 and June 2013 to provide consultation on SDPI. This year, SDPI completed its 15th year providing 404 grants to Indian Health Service, Tribal, and Urban Indian Health (I/T/U) programs across the country.

The SDPI Diabetes Prevention Demonstration Project (DP) grant programs adopted the curriculum from the National Institutes of Health (NIH) Diabetes Prevention Program (DPP).

The SDPI DP achieved a similar low diabetes incidence rate as the original NIH study and published its findings in a major medical journal in July 2013. The SDPI Healthy Heart Demonstration Project (HH) implemented an evidence-based clinical care and case management, which helped reduce risk factors associated with cardiovascular disease. The SDPI DP and HH initiatives grantees, formally the Demonstration Projects, will be disseminating toolkits with materials and resources so other AI/AN communities can implement the programs.

In addition, the SDPI community directed grant programs have provided quality diabetes prevention and treatment services. In 2013, the Diabetes Care and Outcomes Audit, which measures quality and outcomes of diabetes care, audited, 105,626 patient charts at 330 Indian Health facilities. This audit provided the first-ever estimate of cardiovascular disease prevalence in AI/ANs with diabetes compared to the national data. People with diabetes are two to four times more likely to have CVD than people without diabetes.

Of particular importance, rates of new cases of end-stage renal disease (ESRD) in AI/AN people in 2011 were 36 percent lower than they were in 2000 and have decreased more than in other racial and ethnic groups over the past decade. Reduced rates of new cases of ESRD mean a lower rate of people who need to start dialysis.

Combating Childhood Obesity in Indian Country

In February 2010, the First Lady unveiled a nationwide initiative, *Let's Move!*, to fight the epidemic of childhood obesity and improve the health outcomes of children. An integral part of this initiative includes addressing the needs of populations where childhood obesity rates are particularly high, including AI/AN communities. The White House, DOI, Department of Education (ED), USDA, HHS, and the Corporation for National and Community Service came together in May 2011 to launch the *Let's Move! in Indian Country* (*LMIC*) initiative on the Menominee Reservation.

Based on the work of the Childhood Obesity Task Force and the feedback received from tribal leaders, native organizations, urban Indian centers, and others, the *LMIC* interagency partners are focused on the following goals:

1) Creating a healthy start on life;
2) Creating healthy learning communities;
3) Fostering healthy, comprehensive food systems policies; and
4) Increasing opportunities for physical activity.

LMIC is raising awareness about the seriousness of health issues among Native American youth and creating a public/private partnership to build programs that focus on nutrition and exercise. One significant partnership that has grown from the *LMIC* initiative is the Notah Begay III Foundation (NB3 Foundation). NB3 Foundation focuses on improving the health of Native American children across the United States using culturally appropriate, comprehensive, and integrated sports, health, leadership, and community development initiatives.

NB3 Foundation developed a model program at San Felipe Pueblo in Sandoval County, New Mexico, where like in many tribal communities, children experience high rates of childhood obesity and type II diabetes. As part of a two-year study, the Johns Hopkins Center for American

Indian Health researched the impact of three consecutive evaluations from the Foundation's ten-week soccer program. The program was found to have a positive impact on the physical fitness of AI/AN children. NB3 Foundation also pursued a partnership with the Robert Wood Johnson Foundation to become a national center to address childhood obesity and type II diabetes in Native American children. In November, 2013, IHS and NB3 Foundation signed an MOU to collaborate on *LMIC* activities and share best practices on activities that prevent obesity in AI/AN youth.

Improving Subsistence & Food Access Program

The USDA Food Distribution Program on Indian Reservations (FDPIR) provides food to low-income households living on Indian reservations and to American Indian households residing in impoverished areas near reservations in Oklahoma. Many households participate in FDPIR as an alternative to the Supplemental Nutrition Assistance Program (SNAP) because they do not have easy access to SNAP offices or authorized food stores. FDPIR offers a variety of foods to help participants maintain a nutritionally balanced diet.

Federal administrative funding is also available for nutrition education related activities, which can include individual nutrition counseling, cooking demonstrations, nutrition classes, and the dissemination of resources related to USDA. In FY 2013, five states and 100 Indian Tribal Organizations (ITOs) administered FDPIR on 276 Indian reservations, pueblos, rancherias, and Alaska Native Villages. Nutrition assistance was provided to 75,600 participants on an average monthly basis. In addition, in May 2013, USDA Food and Nutrition Service awarded nutrition education grants on a competitive basis to twelve ITOs. The goal of these grants is to enhance nutritional knowledge of FDPIR participants and foster positive lifestyle changes for eligible household members.

Addressing Behavioral Health Issues: Mental Health, Substance Abuse, and Suicide

Many of the behavioral health challenges facing Indian Country are rooted in substance abuse and mental health issues. These issues require a coordinated effort to bring together a variety of resources to help tribal communities and federal technical assistance (TA) services can greatly enhance successful implementation. The Substance Abuse and Mental Health Services Administration (SAMHSA), the Centers for Medicare and Medicaid Services (CMS), and IHS, with federal partners at the Department of Justice (DOJ) and DOI, advanced a collaborative national effort to provide tribal technical assistance to addressing health and safety matters. In May 2013, 8 tribes participated in a Tribal Policy Academy (TPA) on the topic of alternatives to incarceration in Phoenix, Arizona. Building on the success of the discussions at TPA, Federal agencies are planning to provide a program on "Juvenile Alternatives to Incarceration" in spring 2014.

SAMHSA Tribal Training & Technical Assistance Center

In striving to continually improve behavioral health technical assistance services, SAMHSA has awarded a new contract that focuses on AI/AN services through the SAMHSA Tribal Training & Technical Assistance Center (Tribal TTA Center), to promote mental health. The Tribal TTA Center will identify 6-8 AI/AN communities based on data and information related to Native youth violence, substance abuse, bullying, and suicide using socioeconomic, mortality, behavioral health, among other indicators. The Tribal TTA Center compliments the work of the National AI/AN Addiction Technology Transfer Center (AI/AN ATTC), launched last year. The priorities of the AI/AN ATTC include workforce development, the science of addiction, and technology transfer.

SAMHSA Child Mental Health Initiative

The Administration recognizes that the implementation of solutions to behavioral health issues in Indian Country ultimately take place in tribal communities. SAMHSA has several grant programs that provide tribal communities with direct resources and support the development of culturally competent services that are driven by community members. This year SAMHSA awarded six new Child Mental Health Initiative (Systems of Care Program) grants to implement collaborative solutions to improve services and supports for AI/AN youth and their families. Three of the awards support expansion activities for up to three years and three awards fund one-year planning grants to develop a system of care for children with serious mental health challenges and their families. The Circles of Care program targets tribal and urban Indian communities to improve the services for AI/AN youth and their families who are coping with behavioral health issues. The current cohort of Circles of Care tribal grantees is in their second year of a three year grant cycle. Seventy percent of tribal communities are currently receiving grants through the Child Mental Health Initiative were former Circles of Care grantees.

Confronting Suicide in Indian Country

In FY 2013, SAMHSA awarded $2.6 million to two tribal communities specifically for suicide prevention projects. Northwest Indian College is mobilizing a culturally-adapted Model Adolescent Suicide Prevention Program (MASPP) with the Lummi Nation and implementing a suicide surveillance system to assess suicide risks among youth across the seven NWIC campuses (Tulalip, Swinomish, Port Gamble, Muckleshoot, Nisqually, Nez Perce, and Lummi). The Johns Hopkins University, in partnership with the White Mountain Apache tribe, will apply a multi-tiered prevention strategy entitled "Empowering Our Spirits," which includes three culturally adapted, evidence based interventions with a unique community suicide surveillance system serving as a foundation to track change. Primary intervention targets will include: community-wide education to promote protective factors and reduce risks led by elders, early identification and referral of high-risk youth, and intensive outreach to suicidal youth. To date, SAMHSA has funded 57 tribal grants, including 2 tribal colleges through the Garrett Lee Smith Suicide Prevention grant programs.

IHS also administers the Methamphetamine and Suicide Prevention Initiative (MSPI) which supports 130 community-based projects that have implemented a range of culturally tailored suicide prevention initiatives. To date, MSPI accomplishments include:

- Nearly 5,000 individuals entering treatment for methamphetamine abuse;
- Delivery of 7,000 substance abuse and mental health encounters via telehealth;
- More than 7,400 professionals and community members were trained in suicide crisis response; and

- More than 200,000 encounters with at-risk youth were provided with evidence- and practice-based prevention activities.

IHS continues to provide local support by offering a fifth year of funding to Tribes implementing MSPI activities.

Combating Prescription Drug Abuse and Opiate Overdose in Indian Country

Abuse of prescription medications remains a significant public health problem among AI/AN. The Administration has taken significant steps to address the prescription drug abuse epidemic, including the implementation of effective prescription monitoring through state prescription drug monitoring programs (PDMPs). These state-wide databases monitor the prescription and dispensation of controlled substances, serve as a tool for patient care, act as a drug epidemic early warning system, and serve as a drug diversion and insurance fraud investigative tool. Information contained in the PDMP can be used by prescribers and pharmacists to detect and identify patients who may be doctor shopping or in need of substance abuse treatment.

Many tribal boundaries overlap state boundaries, requiring multiple state agreements, increasing the time and difficulty in acquiring PDMP data. IHS, in partnership with DOJ's Bureau of Justice Assistance (BJA), has actively pursued integration with existing state PDMPs since October 2008. BJA and IHS continue to address ongoing challenges around data privacy and reporting requirements to ensure that PDMPs and prescribing data that can be used to address prescription drug abuse and improve care among tribal communities.

The White House Office of National Drug Control Policy is also committed to working with tribal partners to support youth programming to prevent drug use before it begins. In September 2013, ONDCP announced nearly $80 million in grants to more than 600 communities across the country to bolster drug prevention efforts through the Drug-Free Communities Support Program.

Improving Tribal Justice Systems

Tribal Law and Order Act Implementation

The Administration has taken steps to strengthen tribal sovereignty through more effective tribal justice systems. This year marks the three-year anniversary of the enactment of the Tribal Law and Order Act of 2010 (TLOA), and as implementation of the law continues, the TLOA is already improving the Federal Government's ability to work with Indian tribes in the investigation and prosecution of crime impacting tribal communities. This important law gives tribes greater sentencing authority, improves defendants' rights, establishes new guidelines and training for officers handling domestic violence and sexual assault, helps combat alcohol and drug abuse, expands the recruitment and retention of BIA and tribal officers, and gives those officers better access to criminal databases. This year, the Indian Law and Order Commission finished its report and recommended to Congress numerous reforms to improve the provision of justice in Indian country. These reforms are currently under review.

DOJ published its final rule in December 2011 to implement Section 221 of the TLOA, which authorizes the Attorney General to assume concurrent jurisdiction over crimes committed on certain tribal lands. Through this rule, an Indian tribe that is subject to Public Law 280 may request that the Federal government accept concurrent jurisdiction, if the Attorney General consents, Federal authorities can investigate and prosecute criminal offenses within Indian Country. Several tribes have already submitted requests for concurrent Federal criminal jurisdiction. On March 15, 2013, DOJ granted a request by the White Earth Nation for the Federal government to assume concurrent criminal jurisdiction on the 1,300 square miles White Earth Reservation in northern Minnesota. The decision, which was relayed in a letter to the tribe and signed by Deputy Attorney General James Cole, took effect on June 1, 2013. Tribal, state, and county prosecutors and law enforcement agencies will also continue to have criminal jurisdiction on the White Earth Reservation.

Supporting Tribal Enforcement to Combat Drug Trafficking on Tribal Lands

The High Intensity Drug Trafficking Area (HIDTA) Program and ONDCP have been working with tribal authorities to respond to the unique threats faced by Indian Country on drug use and trafficking. HIDTA Programs are well positioned to work with local and tribal communities in order to promote community-based drug prevention programs. HIDTA Programs continue to provide discretionary funds for projects on tribal lands, including funding for task forces, investigations, training, and prevention efforts in the California Central Valley, New York/New Jersey, North Texas, Northwest, Oregon, Southwest Border-Arizona, North Dakota and Montana's Bakken Region, and Southwest Border-New Mexico.

Currently, ONDCP is working with Federal law enforcement partners with equities in Indian Country—the Departments of Homeland Security and DOJ—to better coordinate and leverage Federal resources. The group will expand to include non-law enforcement entities in the near future as ONDCP convenes stakeholders to ensure that drug use and its consequences are addressed with both public safety and public health tactics.

Supporting Tribal Justice Systems

In February 2010, DOJ announced a streamlined approach for AI/AN tribes to apply for funding opportunities. The Coordinated Tribal Assistance Solicitation ("CTAS") serves as a single application for existing tribal government-specific grant programs administered by the Office of Justice Programs ("OJP"), Community Oriented Policing Services ("COPS"), and the Office on Violence Against Women ("OVW"). DOJ awarded $127 million in CTAS grants to more than 130 American Indian and Alaska Native nations in September 2010, more than $118 million in CTAS grants to more than 150 American Indian and Alaska Native nations in September 2011, more than $101 million in CTAS grants to more than 110 American Indian and Alaska Native nations in September 2012, and more than $90 million to 110 American Indian tribes, Alaska Native villages, tribal consortia and tribal designated non-profits in September 2013.

DOJ's Access to Justice Initiative (ATJ) and the BIA's OJS co-sponsored an expert group meeting in April 2013 on the use of traditional Native American justice practices to respond to criminal and delinquent behavior. The one-day roundtable meeting brought together leaders and experts on the use of traditional justice practices to discuss the benefits and challenges of these programs and processes and developed recommendations to the Federal Government on how to support these practices. ATJ and OJS are preparing a report summarizing the expert group's discussions and recommendations, which will be disseminated to tribal criminal justice stakeholders in furtherance of the TLOA's mandate that both Departments help tribes develop alternatives to incarceration.

Additionally, BIA contracted with independent tribal companies to conduct tribal court reviews. Tribal court reviews are intended to assist the BIA Office of Justice Services (OJS) in providing specific technical assistance and training needed by individual tribal judicial systems. Twenty tribal judicial systems are currently being reviewed and receiving additional funding. These reviews highlight areas needing technical assistance and training sessions in 2014.

Reducing Violent Crime Through High Priority Performance Goal Initiative

The Office of Justice Services witnessed great success during the first Safe Indian Communities, High Priority Performance Goal (HPPG) initiative, which was implemented at four reservations with elevated violent crime rates. The goal of the HPPG initiative was to achieve significant reduction in criminal offenses, by at least 5 percent within 24 months, through the implementation of a comprehensive strategy involving community policing, tactical deployment, and critical interagency and intergovernmental partnerships. The overall impact of the baseline year 2009 versus current 2013 statistics is as follows:

Rocky Boys Reservation	- 52%
Mescalero Apache Reservation	- 91%
Standing Rock Reservation	- 37%
Wind River Reservation	- 60%

To expand the success to other areas of Indian Country, OJS selected two additional reservations to implement the HPPG initiative. The Rosebud Sioux Tribe in South Dakota and San Carlos Apache Tribe in Arizona were selected based upon violent crime rates above the national average.

Using the information obtained during a community assessment, an action plan was developed that is comprised of best practices to implement sustained crime reduction in each community. The plan includes customized community policing programs to ensure the best level of success; strategic operation practices tailored to the community for stronger patrol and enforcement within current staffing levels; enhancement of tribal court procedures and operations; and establishment and mediation of any necessary partnerships with various federal, state and local programs such as the Drug Enforcement Administration ("DEA") or drug task forces, social services, and rehabilitation programs.

This year, OJS also created the "HPPG Best Practices Handbook" that serves as a compilation of the strategies that proved to be instrumental in achieving reduction in violent crime. The best practices identified in the handbook are guidelines for law enforcement entities operating throughout Indian Country. The findings were drawn from several sources, including individual interviews conducted with the police chiefs and command staff of each HPPG reservation, a focus group session, demographic data that profiled each HPPG reservation and its citizens, and documentation submitted by the four reservations.

Veterans Justice Outreach

The purpose of the Veterans Justice Outreach (VJO) Program is to avoid the unnecessary criminalization of mental illness and extended incarceration among Veterans by ensuring that eligible justice-involved Veterans have timely access to VHA services as clinically indicated. Veterans Justice Outreach Specialists are responsible for direct outreach, assessment, and case management for justice-involved Veterans in local courts and jails, and liaison with local justice system partners. The VA Office of Tribal Government Relations worked closely with the Bureau of Indian Affairs-Office of Tribal Justice Services to provide training to tribal judges in locations throughout the country.

VA continues to partner closely with the Tribal Veterans' community and administers the Veterans Cemetery Grants Program (VCGP), which provides grants to states and tribal organizations for up to 100 percent of the cost of establishing, expanding, or improving State and Tribal Veterans Cemeteries. To date, VA has awarded a total of five grants to tribal organizations for the construction of new Veterans cemeteries on tribal trust lands as authorized by law. VA awarded one additional grant to a tribal organization in FY 2013 to the Seminole Nation of Oklahoma and is currently engaging with Tribal Organizations on five new tribal pre-applications submitted for funding consideration in FY 2014. In addition, VA dedicated a new cemetery to veterans on the Rosebud Sioux Reservation.

Combating Violence Against Native Women

IHS administers the Domestic Violence Prevention Initiative (DVPI) which supports 65 community-based projects implementing a range of culturally tailored domestic and sexual violence prevention initiatives. To date, DVPI accomplishments include:

- Over 151,000 screenings for domestic violence and 11,000 referrals for service;
- More than 19,000 individuals received crisis intervention, victim advocacy, case management, and counseling services;
- Nearly 6,000 professionals were trained at 478 training events; and
- 344 sexual assault forensic evidence collection kits were submitted to Federal, State, and Tribal law enforcement.

In 2013, IHS also launched its tribal forensic healthcare website, which offers training on domestic and sexual violence to medical providers through webinars and a web-based learning system. Additionally, 46 IHS and tribal hospitals and clinics received equipment to aid in the clinical documentation and evidentiary collection during sexual assault medical forensic examinations.

U.S. Attorney's Offices' Tribal Engagement

U.S. Attorneys from 30 of 49 districts with Indian Country serve on the Attorney General's Advisory Council (AGAC) Native American Issues Subcommittee (NAIS). The NAIS focuses exclusively on Indian Country issues, both criminal and civil, and is responsible for making policy recommendations to the Attorney General regarding public safety and legal issues. In September 2013, Associate Attorney General Tony West, the NAIS, and officials from the Environment and Natural Resources Division and the Office of Tribal Justice met with tribes in the Pacific Northwest to discuss issues of public safety, hunting and fishing rights, and other issues of interest to the tribes.

American Indian/Alaska Native Children Exposed to Violence Task Force

In August 2013, the Department of Justice launched a new initiative, the American Indian/Alaska Native Children Exposed to Violence Task Force, which is dedicated to addressing the unique challenges faced by children in Indian Country. This task force is a key part of the Department's Defending Childhood Initiative – to prevent and reduce children's trauma from experiencing violence as victims or witnesses – that reported that American Indian and Alaska Native children experience high degrees of unmet needs for services and support to prevent and respond to extreme levels of violence.

The Task Force is made up of an Advisory Committee of tribal members and national experts – in academia, child health and trauma, and child welfare and law – and a Working Group that includes U.S. Attorneys and officials from the Departments of Justice, the Interior, and Health and Human Services.

The Advisory Committee has been appointed to examine the scope and impact of violence facing American Indian and Alaska Native children and make policy recommendations to Attorney General Holder on ways to address this issue. The Working Group was formed to support the Advisory Committee because the Department recognizes that there are things we can do right now that can have a direct and immediate impact in children's lives. Since its inception in August, the Working Group of federal officials has taken action to improve educational and programmatic services in youth detention facilities in Indian Country.

Over this next year, the Advisory Committee will travel throughout country, holding hearings and listening sessions. The Advisory Committee will explore existing research and consult with experts to obtain a clearer picture of the incidence of violence among native children, and help identify ways to prevent it. The Advisory Committee's work will culminate in a final report – a strategic plan of action that will guide practitioners and policymakers at all levels. Similar to the work of the Defending Childhood Task Force, the recommendations of the Advisory Committee will serve as a blueprint to guide us into the future.

Expanding and Improving Educational Opportunities

This Administration is working with tribes to achieve a brighter future for AI/AN students by developing efforts that will reduce unemployment across tribal nations and promote economic growth in Indian Country. In 2013, the Administration proposed changes to enhance the role of tribes in the education of their youth, in response to tribal leaders' desire for greater control over the education of AI/AN students. The Administration also provided greater flexibility in the use of Federal funds to meet the unique needs of AI/AN students.

Improving American Indian and Alaska Native Educational Opportunities

The White House Initiative on American Indian and Alaska Native Education has taken a number of significant steps in 2013 to implement the President's Executive Order 13592,

Improving American Indian and Alaska Native Education Opportunities and Strengthening Tribal Colleges and Universities.

A DOI-ED Joint Committee on Indian Education, which includes tribal leader representatives from the Tribal Interior Budget Council, is working to develop an action plan that leverages the expertise of each department to implement the seven goals and specific activities of a 2012 DOI-ED Memorandum of Understanding (MOU). The President's Interagency Working Group on Indian Education convened its inaugural meeting on February 7, 2013, bringing together Senior Administration Officials from 29 federal agencies to begin interagency implementation of the President's Executive Order. The development of the federal agencies' two-part, four-year plans are underway, and will focus on expanding educational opportunities and improving outcomes for AI/AN students, including helping to ensure that AI/AN students have an opportunity to learn their native Languages.

On August 8, 2013, Secretary Duncan and Secretary Jewell visited the Wind River Indian Reservation in Wyoming. The Secretaries heard directly from tribal leaders and school officials about the concerns and efforts needed to address the unique needs of AI/AN students. The visit marked the first time in history the Secretaries of Education and Interior visited Indian Country together.

Secretary Jewell and Secretary Duncan visit the Wind River Indian Reservation in furtherance of the White House Initiative on American Indian and Alaska Native Education Opportunities.
(Department of Education Photo)

Family Education Rights & Privacy Act

To further tribal self-determination and provide access to critical decision-making data, BIE created a Family Education Rights and Privacy Act Agreement (FERPA) allowing tribes, as authorized representatives, to access student information data at their BIE funded schools. These agreements further our efforts to improve student performance by strengthening information access and data sharing at the tribal level. BIE signed its first FERPA Agreement with the Navajo Nation on November 12, 2013.

Supporting Tribal Colleges and Universities

The Department of Education (ED) provided approximately $138.3 million to tribal colleges and universities (TCUs) in FY 2012. This funding was dedicated to four activities: (1) improving and strengthening the academic quality, institutional management, and fiscal stability of TCUs; (2) grants and loan assistance authorized under Title IV of the Higher Education Act (HEA) to help TCU students pay for college; (3) grants designed to prepare and train AI/ANs to serve as teachers and education professionals; and (4) grants to Federally-recognized Indian tribes, tribal organizations, Alaska Native entities and eligible BIE funded schools to improve career and technical education (CTE) programs for AI/ANs.

BIE has initiated a series of significant steps for strengthening the role of BIE-funded institutions of higher education (Haskell Indian Nations University and Southwestern Indian Polytechnic Institute, or SIPI). Progress is also being made toward creating new and expanded partnerships between Federal agencies, such as the National Park Service and OJS, and TCUs.

Dr. Jill Biden walks with the procession of graduates of the Navajo Technical College Class of 2013, Navajo Tech President Elmer Guy, Navajo Nation President Ben Shelly and the Board of trustees on the Navajo Tech campus in Crownpoint, New Mexico. May 17, 2013. *(Official White House Photo by Chuck Kennedy)*

USDA National Institute for Food and Agriculture (NIFA) manages four USDA funding programs for TCUs: the Tribal Colleges Research Grants program, the Tribal Colleges Education Equity Grants program, the 1994 Tribal Colleges Extension Grants program, and the 1994 Tribal Colleges Endowment program. In 2013, thirty-two TCUs with land grant status received approximately $13.2 million in grant award funds. NIFA also provided support to the Federally Recognized Tribal Extension Program, funding 36 awards in the amount of $2.7 million to provide essential youth development and agriculture development services at the tribal level. Together, these programs provided funds for 96 student scholarships, 119 student internships, 21 distance education programs, and 22 GIS related projects. In addition, NIFA served approximately 54,000 youth with after school nutrition and natural resource education programs. USDA Rural Development also provided 24 grants totaling $3 million to TCUs under its Community Facilities program.

In November 2013, over one hundred professors and students from the Land Grant TCUs came to USDA's Waterfront Center in Washington, D.C. for their annual conference. This annual meeting, sponsored by the First American Land Grant Consortium, is hosted by NIFA every four years. NIFA set up a special panel where leaders and senior faculty from the tribal colleges shared the barriers they face in participating in NIFA grant programs with USDA senior leadership. A special follow up session was held with the TCU leaders and leadership from NIFA's grant programs related to water quality, climate change, health and rural development. The program leadership talked one-on-one with tribal college faculty and provided mentoring that NIFA hopes will increase program participation.

Alaska Native Serving and Native Hawaiian Serving Institutions Competitive Grants Program

USDA's NIFA administers the Native Hawaiian and Alaska Native Serving Institutions Education Competitive Grants Program (ANNH), which provides funding for colleges and universities that provide Native Hawaiian and Alaska Native students with educational and career opportunities within a broadly defined area of food and agricultural sciences and related disciplines. In FY 2013, ANNH awarded $2.8 million to a consortium of 9 institutions in the University of Hawaii system; a consortium of 5 institutions in the University of Alaska system; and one individual award to the University of Alaska Southeast. ANNH supported more than 1200 students from 2012-2013. 2013 projects included agri-business, aquaculture, food and nutritional science education, and extension programs for community development. This program has awarded more than $39.7 million since its creation in 2001.

Increased Technical Assistance and Capacity Building

The Office of Indian Education (OIE) at ED provided approximately $993,000 in FY 2012 funds to three Regional Comprehensive Centers to improve outcomes for AI/AN students by providing technical assistance to state educational agencies (SEA). This support will amount to nearly $5 million of technical assistance services, including working with States to help them gain a better understanding of the issues and challenges facing AI/AN students, building cultural competency among staff, and delivering instruction that is culturally appropriate for students.

ED also continues to partner with the National Indian Education Association, the largest member organization of AI/AN educators and advocates in the country, to deliver high quality technical assistance during their annual convention. The fourth annual ED Technical Assistance Day, *"Strong Partnerships, Successful Students,"* brought over 300 AI/AN educators and advocates together with ED Senior Officials and program staff to engage on the Administration's reform agenda, initiatives, programs, and funds available to support AI/AN students.

Post-9/11 GI Bill Opportunities

VA provides education benefits to eligible service members, veterans, dependents and survivors. One of our education programs, the Post-9/11 GI Bill, provides payment for tuition and fees, books and supplies, and housing allowance. Qualified Native veterans may receive financial support for undergraduate and graduate degrees, vocational and technical training, licensing and certification tests, apprenticeships, and on-the-job training.

Increasing Education Outreach and Support to Indian Communities

Department of Education Formula Competitive Grants

The Administration has demonstrated strong support for Native American students through formula and competitive grants to help meet their unique needs. In FY 2012-2013, ED awarded Title VII formula program funds to 1,302 grants in 23 states, totaling approximately $106 million. Additionally, Title VII Special Programs for Indian Children Demonstration and Professional Development awarded grants totaling approximately $19.2 million to support programs that offer early learning, transition to college, and degree opportunities for teachers and administrators.

State-Tribal Education Partnership (STEP) Program

Under the State-Tribal Education Partnership (STEP) Program in 2013, ED made continuation awards to four tribal education agencies (TEAs) totaling approximately $1.6 million dollars. These TEAs have developed agreements with their State Educational Agency partners to foster greater involvement of Tribes in the education of AI/AN students attending public schools on tribal lands.

Promise Neighborhoods Program

The Administration has secured $100 million over the past three years to develop Promise Neighborhoods and provide communities with a continuum of services, from "cradle to career," to meet educational challenges. In 2011, ED added a priority for tribal communities to the program and awarded the Campo Band of Mission Indians a $500,000 Promise Neighborhoods planning grant.

The following year, the priority was used again for the Promise Neighborhoods grant competition and the Paskenta Band of Nomlaki Indians was awarded $500,000 for the Everett Freeman Initiative (EFI). The EFI is a Promise Neighborhood Planning Grant Project that is a grass-roots, collaborative undertaking by all the stakeholders in the Corning-Paskenta Tribal Community. EFI's vision is that all children and youth growing up in the Corning-Paskenta Tribal area will attend schools of excellence that are bolstered by strong family, tribal, and community support systems that will prepare them to attain an excellent education and successfully transition them to college and a career.

National Advisory Council on Indian Education

The President's National Advisory Council on Indian Education (NACIE) met four times this year and released a report to Congress in June 2013. The fifteen-member Council advises the Secretary of ED on the funding and administration of any program under the Secretary's jurisdiction, makes recommendations to the Secretary on filling the position of Director of Indian Education, and reports to Congress recommendations for improving Federal education programs that benefit Native Americans.

Protection of Native American Lands and the Environment, and Respect for Cultural Rights

The Administration is committed to protecting human health and the environment, consulting on environmental issues affecting tribes, and recognizing that many indigenous peoples depend upon a healthy environment for subsistence fishing, hunting, and gathering. In furtherance of this goal, the Administration has taken many steps to ensure the protection of Native American lands and natural resources.

Protecting Tribal Lands

U.S. Geological Service

This year, the U.S. Geological Service (USGS) led an effort to ensure that the National Climate Assessment reports included tribal lands and communities for the very first time, with a comprehensive review of the impacts and adaptation efforts of tribes in the Southwest. This work, as well as other USGS research, helped raise awareness regarding the contributions of traditional knowledge to understanding climate change impacts in regions of the United States outside Alaska. Continuing work on the impact of climate change to Tribes in the Southwestern United States includes an examination of increasing temperatures on drought impacts, their effects on Navajo rangeland, and possible management strategies to mitigate these impacts.

The USGS National Climate Change and Wildlife Science Center convened the initial meeting of a Tribal and Indigenous Knowledge Working Group, under the auspices of the newly established Advisory Committee on Climate Change and Natural Resource Science (ACCCNRS). The Group, which contains tribal representation, is developing a work plan for tribal/indigenous matters for ACCCNRS, focusing initially on tribal climate science needs, effective communication between Federal climate science efforts and tribes, capacity gaps in Indian country, and traditional/local ecological knowledge.

The USGS Coastal and Marine Geology Program and Coastal Habitats in Puget Sound Project continue to work with Tribes to advance ecosystem restoration, climate change adaptation, and coastal and marine spatial planning across the Pacific Northwest. These efforts are funded by several tribes, USEPA, USGS, the USGS Northwest Climate Science Center and DOI North

Pacific Landscape Conservation Cooperative and provide fundamental research and training to help build capacity within Indian Country. The project completed its 6th annual survey helping federal, tribal, state, and local agencies monitor and understand the changing conditions of the Salish Sea that affect first foods and traditional ways.

Implementing Environmental Policy

The Environmental Protection Agency (EPA) Consultation Policy establishes a broad standard regarding the type of EPA actions and decisions that may warrant consultation. In 2013, EPA concluded two rounds of tribal consultation and coordination and released new General Assistance Program (GAP) grant guidance. GAP represents the single largest source of financial support the EPA provides to tribal governments and helps build tribal government capacity to administer their own environmental programs consistent with Federal environmental standards and regulations. The new GAP guidance strengthens fiscal management, improves pre-award GAP grant work plan negotiations with tribes, and provides a nationally consistent framework for measuring tribal environmental protection program capacity. The guidance also helps EPA establish a foundation for effective program implementation in Indian country and helps tribes identify the appropriate pathways for their environmental priorities.

EPA is also working with tribal governments to increase administrative flexibility under the Agency's grant programs. For example in January 2013, EPA and the Corporation for National and Community Service continued their agreement to allow tribes to use EPA's Indian Environmental (GAP) grant funds as match funding for tribally-sponsored AmeriCorps programs. More than $3 million of AmeriCorps funding is dedicated to support tribal communities every year, but tribal governments often face financial challenges that prevent them from matching the required funding. This partnership will reduce those barriers for many tribes and will lead to projects that help tribes expand services, build capacity, and create sustainable programs. EPA senior leadership has made a commitment to developing more of these partnerships, and created an intra-agency workgroup focused on using grant funding to provide environmental protection in Indian country.

Implementing the National Ocean Policy

In 2013, the National Ocean Council released the National Ocean Policy Implementation Plan and Marine Planning Handbook, which emphasizes the importance of respecting the government-to-government relationship with Federally-recognized tribes and invites participation of interested tribes in regional marine planning efforts. Four regional planning bodies (RPBs) were officially established in the Northeast, Mid-Atlantic, Pacific Islands, and Caribbean regions, with several tribes serving as members of the Northeast and Mid-Atlantic RPBs. Tribal outreach about the National Ocean Policy and marine planning continues in other regions, which have expressed an interest in forming regional planning bodies. The National Ocean Council's Governance Coordinating Committee, which includes three tribal members selected to represent tribal interests nationally, continues to provide valuable insight, guidance, and assistance to the National Ocean Council on the implementation of the National Ocean Policy.

Respect for Cultural Rights

The President recognizes that the indigenous peoples of North America have invaluable cultural knowledge and rich traditions, which continue to thrive in Native American communities across the country. The activities of many federal agencies impact these cultures and traditions, and several have taken formal steps to institutionalize respect for the rights of Native American communities and their traditions.

United Nations Declaration on the Rights of Indigenous Peoples

At the 2010 White House Tribal Nations Conference, the President announced that the United States supports the U.N. Declaration of Rights of Indigenous Peoples, reversing the decision of the U.S. in 2007 to vote against the Declaration. However, the Administration does not see support for the Declaration as an end in itself. In the President's words, "[w]hat matters far more than words—what matters far more than any resolution or declaration—are actions to match those words." Accordingly, ACHP adopted a plan to support the U.N. Declaration by unanimous vote on March 1, 2013.

Protection of Sacred Sites and Repatriation of Human Remains and Cultural Items

The Bureau of Land Management (BLM) s working with tribes to facilitate the reburial of repatriated Native American ancestors on BLM public lands in areas with limited risk of future disturbances and are also easily accessible to tribes. BLM works with tribes to identify ways that objects recovered through law enforcement activities can be used to educate the public on the problem of looting sites on public lands and the cultural losses to tribes when such looting occurs. The goal is to help ensure that traditional sites and burials remain undistributed and that cultural objects do not fall into the hands of private collectors.

Native American Grants and Repatriation Act

In FY 2013, 21 grants were awarded pursuant to the Native American Grants and Repatriation Act (NAGPRA) by the National Park Services (NPS) for projects supporting consultation between tribes and museums leading to claims for cultural items, and 13 NAGPRA grants were awarded for costs of repatriation of Native American human remains and cultural items from museums and Federal agencies to tribes and NHOs, in the total amount of $1,628,906. From 1994 to 2013, $39,870,597 has been awarded in NAGPRA grants. A proposed rule was published to address the unclaimed Native American human remains and newly discovered funerary objects on Federal lands after the date of NAGPRA's enactment. New discoveries on Federal and Indian land do not result in additions to collections, but under NAGPRA, are subject to prompt disposition to tribes. The new rule provides options for additional consultations and disposition, including reburial, for those unclaimed. The comment period on the proposed rule closed on December 30, 2013.

Bureau of Ocean Energy Management

The Bureau of Ocean Energy Management's (BOEM) Pacific Outer Continental Shelf (OCS) Region is funding a collaborative effort with National Oceanic and Atmospheric Administration's Office of National Marine Sanctuaries, the National Marine Protected Areas Center, Tribal Facilitators, and the Tribal Historic Preservation Offices (THPOs) of the Yurok Tribe, Confederated Tribes of Grand Ronde, and the Makah Tribe. The project is designed to develop an approach to work with Native American communities to identify areas of tribal significance that need consideration in the planning process for future offshore renewable energy development. Information from this project will facilitate decision-making processes that consider the importance of these locales, and give tribal communities a more effective voice during regional energy planning. In support of this effort, each THPO hosted an inter-tribal workshop to bring together neighboring tribes, as well as state and Federal agency representatives with ties to the coast, to develop an analysis guide for the project.

BOEM is also funding a partnership between the University of Rhode Island and the Narragansett Indian Tribe to develop protocols for reconstructing paleocultural landscapes and identifying ancient Native American sites in submerged environments. The project is the first of its kind and attempts to integrate Western scientific methods with a nuanced understanding of tribal oral traditions to gain a better predict where tribal ancestors would have lived on lands. Part of the project is also training young tribal members in the science of remote-sensing and archaeology needed to understand where submerged and burial ancestral sites may have survived global sea level rise resulting from the melting glaciers following the last ice age.

Interagency Sacred Sites Memorandum of Understanding

Tribal leaders raised concerns about the destruction of sacred sites during several Tribal Nations Conferences. In response to these concerns, DOI, USDA, DOD, and DOE and the Advisory Council on Historic Preservation (ACHP) entered into a memorandum of understanding (MOU) on December 5, 2012, to work collaboratively to address the protection of and Indian access to sacred sites. The MOU required signatories to develop an action plan and on March 5, 2013, the plan was released and implementation began immediately. There have been extensive outreach efforts including the development of a website. The signatories began collecting information about training and management practices and analyzing federal statutes and executive orders related to sacred sites protection. A report documenting the signatories' progress in implementing the MOU and Action Plan will be released in mid-January.

The Preservation of Native Languages

In 2013, the Administration took significant steps to promote the preservation and revitalization of native languages in both primary and post-secondary education. To address the need to remove barriers for early childhood education programs, ACF will be issuing an Information Memorandum to all ACF early childhood programs that will clarify cost principles related to sharing resources and programming across offices, highlighting ways these programs can come together to share language and cultural instruction. In addition, the agencies are exploring possibilities for a Native American Languages Summit in 2014.

For FY 2014, the Office of Postsecondary Education included an Invitational Priority to support activities that strengthen Native language preservation and revitalization in institutions of higher education in the Title III Alaska Native and Native Hawaiian-Serving Institutions grant competition. Moreover, BIE made several important changes to the application for Title VII formula grants for FY 2014 in order to emphasize the statutory requirement that grant funds be used as part of a comprehensive program for meeting the culturally-related academic needs of Indian students, including the language and cultural needs of the children. In 2013, there were approximately 1,300 Title VII programs and 500,000 students served nationwide. In 2013, the South Central Comprehensive Center, one of three ED Regional Comprehensive Centers, supported the Oklahoma State Department of Education in the development of the native language certification and is continuing to provide technical assistance during statewide implementation of an alternate pathway in native language certification. This work addresses the critical need for fluent native language instructors to be involved in efforts to enhance native language revitalization among tribes.

Federal Acknowledgment

This year, BIA continued its comprehensive review of the tribal federal acknowledgment process. DOI released a discussion draft on potential revisions to the 25 CFR Part 83 regulation, which outlines federal acknowledgement criterion. DOI received approximately 350 comment submissions over the span of three months from a wide array of stakeholders. DOI is currently reviewing the comments it received and plans to proceed with a proposed rule for publication in the Federal Register. The Agency will open a second round of consultation as well as the formal comment period prior to the publication of the final rule.

www.ingramcontent.com/pod-product-compliance
Lightning Source LLC
Chambersburg PA
CBHW080613290526
45790CB00007B/2757